Pray Now

2013

Daily Devotions on the Theme of Generation to Generation

Published on behalf of the
THE PRAY NOW GROUP

SAINT ANDREW PRESS
Edinburgh

First published in 2012 by
Saint Andrew Press
121 George Street
Edinburgh EH2 4YN

Copyright © Pray Now Group, Faith Expressions Team, Mission and Discipleship Council, The Church of Scotland, 2012

ISBN 978 0 86153 624 5

British Library Cataloguing in Publication Data
A catalogue record for this book is available from the British Library

It is the publisher's policy to only use papers that are natural and recyclable and that have been manufactured from timber grown in renewable, properly managed forests. All of the manufacturing processes of the papers are expected to conform to the environmental regulations of the country of origin.

Typeset in Times by Waverley Typesetters, Warham
Printed and bound by CPI Group (UK) Ltd, Croydon, CR0 4YY

Contents

Preface   v

Using this Book   vi

Days of the Month

Day 1	Abraham, Isaac and Jacob	2
Day 2	David	4
Day 3	Elizabeth, Zechariah and John the Baptist	6
Day 4	James, John and Zebedee	8
Day 5	Simon and his Mother-in-Law	10
Day 6	Martha and her Sister Mary	12
Day 7	The Devil	14
Day 8	Queen of Sheba	16
Day 9	Herod and Herodias	18
Day 10	Pharisees	20
Day 11	Lawyers	22
Day 12	Mary Magdalene, Joanna, Susanna and Many Others	24
Day 13	Joseph of Arimathea	26
Day 14	Boaz and Ruth	28
Day 15	The Shepherds	30
Day 16	The Haemorrhaging Woman	32
Day 17	The Poor Widow	34
Day 18	Zacchaeus	36
Day 19	The Man Beaten up on the Road to Jericho	38

Day 20	His Servant Israel	40
Day 21	Jacob	42
Day 22	Elijah	44
Day 23	Solomon	46
Day 24	Mary	48
Day 25	Jesus	50
Day 26	Theophilus	52
Day 27	The Eleven Disciples	54
Day 28	Cleopas and his Companion	56
Day 29	Jairus' Daughter	58
Day 30	The Little Child Placed in the Centre	60
Day 31	Us	62

The Months

January	New Beginnings	66
February	Love	68
March	Lent	70
April	Eastertide	72
May	Holy Spirit	74
June	Generations	76
July	Holidays	78
August	Festivals	80
September	Learning	82
October	Harvest	84
November	Remembrance	86
December	Edges and Extremes	88

Using Pray Now 2013 *as a Worship Resource*   90

Pray Now 2013 *Daily Lectionary*   94

Acknowledgements   113

Contact Us   114

Preface

Have humans gone deaf? Does this generation have ears to hear God's Song? It is a song constantly sung through creation, sometimes with words, sometimes in silence, but always with longing and patience for a world reborn through justice and freedom. Creation recognizes it new every morning, the poor hear it, the hungry are familiar with it, the proud perhaps wish to be deaf to it and the mighty try to shout over it, but they can't.

Pray Now this year invites you into that song through prayer and reflection. Taking themes born from the Magnificat, God's Own Song that has been sung down the generations, we invite you to sing with those who have sung it before us: past generations opening the ears of this generation. This is a great timeless community called to keep those longings of God: justice, freedom, full lives for the oppressed and imprisoned, alive through our living a prayerful life.

I hope you hear God's Song through these pages and find the space and the time to accompany Mary in the Magnificat and all those characters who join her in Luke's Gospel and in every generation that has given voice, even just a note or two, to live out and make known God's Dream in our prayer. It is quite a chorus.

REVD RODDY HAMILTON
Vice-Convener
Faith Expression Team 2013
Mission and Discipleship Council

Using this Book

'His mercy is for those who fear him from generation to generation.'

~ Luke 1:50 ~

This year's theme is 'Generations'. We give thanks for all we have learned and gained from past generations. We think of the different age generations of our present times and we do so recognizing our responsibility as God's trustees of the world for future generations. Underpinning all our praying is a humble acknowledgement that we stand in the line of the generations of the Spirit through which God has called and commissioned His people throughout time.

The 'Pray Now' Writing Group identified the theme from the inspirational passage 'The Magnificat' – Mary's song of praise and justice. We have read 'The Magnificat' in the context of the whole of Luke's Gospel account believing that God's saving work is still happening across the generations. The passage is a continuing call for justice and freedom for the poor, the oppressed, the imprisoned and those who live in darkness.

The main part of the book is in the pattern of previous years with thirty-one days of prayerful stimuli. Each day is titled by one or more characters that appear in the Gospel of Luke. We classified each of these characters within one of the groups mentioned in 'The Magnificat':

- **Generations – Days 1–6**

  We explore the importance of our forefathers and of family groups in passing the faith on to the next generation.

- **The Proud, the Powerful and the Rich –**
  Days 7–13

  We see that pride, power and riches can be used for destructive purposes or for transformational and creative work in God's name.

- **The Lowly and the Hungry – Days 14–19**

  We reflect on how God favours and uses the poor and the humble for his messengers and as beacons of faith.

- **His Servants – Days 20–25**

  We look at how God can use nations, kings, prophets, ordinary men and women and his own Son/Self to bring about His rule on earth.

- **Disciples – Days 26–31**

  We meditate on how Jesus used children and adults to teach the disciples about His identity and mission as well as looking at the disciples themselves. This part of the book closes with reflection about our own discipleship and church mission today.

Each day contains the following:

- a biblical verse that has stimulated the content for the day
- a short meditation
- a short prayer
- two suggestions for scriptural reading
- a blessing.

Each day may be taken as a whole, or readers may choose to reflect only on the meditation to prompt personal prayer and next month use the suggested prayer for reflection.

The second part of the book is a new addition. We have included twelve monthly prayers. You may wish to pray that prayer every day of the month and focus on a different aspect of the intercession each day or week. The addition of the monthly prayers offers an opportunity to use *Pray Now* morning and evening.

There are also prayer activities offered, which are suitable for all ages, friends or other groups who wish to pray together. Therefore the monthly prayer can become a cross-generational activity and involve a practical project. The monthly pages finish with a short prayer written by a renowned theologian or literary figure chosen from across the generations of writings.

Prayer is like the breath of the soul. Sometimes it is almost subconscious but it is also helpful to set aside time for more focused prayers. Many people use *Pray Now* as an aid to their personal devotions, praying in a chosen place at home or work or outside or while travelling. The material may also be used as stimuli for:

- prayer pairs or a prayer group – in a home or church or via a social networking site such as Facebook
- midweek or shorter acts of worship with the addition of a hymn and perhaps a discussion element (see pp. 90–93)
- as opening devotions at the beginning of a meeting such as Guild or Kirk Session Meeting
- meditations may also be used in main acts of worship if they help the congregation to explore or reflect on one of the Bible readings for the day
- a summer series preaching on the themes of 'The Magnificat' could utilize some of the content of this year's *Pray Now*.

In whatever way you choose to use the book the writing group hope that it helps you pray with and live out 'The Magnificat'.

'And Mary said, "My soul magnifies the Lord".' Surely whenever we pray our souls magnify the Lord? It is a lovely thought that in various ways, our lives too can be like a lens that increases the size of God's presence on earth and makes God's work easier to see. It is good to realize that every act of generosity, compassion, justice and love magnifies the Lord.

May you grow the Lord well.

REVD CAROL FORD
Convener of the Pray Now *Writing Group 2013*

Days of the Month

ABRAHAM, ISAAC AND JACOB

God is able from these stones to raise up children to Abraham.

~ Luke 3:8 ~

Meditation

Fathers for Justice,
beleaguered boys cloaked as men,
dressed as Batman and Robin
clumsily clambering up public buildings.
Ridiculous really, how things have changed.

We yearn for the Fathers of previous generations
and we call out to you, Abraham, Isaac and Jacob.
Fathers of justice,
rooted in something so much more tangible
than a cry for recognition on a rooftop.
We call to you, for you are our ancestral fathers,
rooted in faith and a love that transcends generations.

We are all children of Abraham.
We will never know the true sacrifice in Isaac
and the scars of family feuding
are bound whole in Jacob's wrestle
for reconciliation.

Abraham, Isaac and Jacob,
you bring us close to how fatherhood might be.
You raise us up as children to God,
who is so much more than our Father.

Hallowed be your name.

Prayer

God of all Fathers,
We call to You in this our generation
looking for reassurance that all is not lost
that Your love transcends generations
from the Patriarchs of the Old Testament

to men of the here and now;
guide us, lead us,
raise us up,
nurture us, and yes, mother us, too
until Your kingdom come,
Your will be done.   Amen.

Suggested Readings

Genesis 32   *Jacob's encounter with Esau and God*
Acts 3   *Peter in the Temple*

Blessing

May God who is more than Mother, more than Father,
bless to you this day.
May you find the belonging of an ancestral home
and may you find reconciliation and wholeness,
today and every day.   Amen.

DAVID

And David came to Saul and entered his service. Saul loved him greatly, and he became his armour-bearer.

~ 1 Samuel 16:21 ~

Meditation

Sing a song of loyalty
with the flock upon the hillside, standing open to the wild;
entering the service of a master, consumed by inner turmoil;
for the people,
who will place their trust in a usurper.

Sing a song of bravery
shown in battles fought with lion
and with bear;
played out when standing
where no other stood,
against a giant;
in flight,
when the one in whom you trusted
no longer trusts in you.

Sing a song of passion
as faithful devotion to God is revealed in service and song;
through the emotions that are plundered in the torn
    relationships
of man and woman,
king and captain,
God and servant.

Sing a song of penitence
when the servant fails the people;
for the relationships betrayed;
as the recognition of human need
is met in the forgiving love of God.

Prayer

Music Master,
inspiring the song within,
may my voice
share the passions of the Gospel
and stir the emotions
that lead to justice and love.
May the lyrics
reveal Your presence
in the lives of those
who know You in their joy,
encounter You in solitude,
and seek You in their distress.
May the music
welcome new rhythms
as Your Spirit moves creation
from the familiar
to a different pace and knowledge.   AMEN.

Suggested Readings

    1 Samuel 16:14–23   *David comes to serve Saul*
    2 Samuel 1:17–27   *David's lament over Saul and*
                                 Jonathan

Blessing

In the songs of life
may I hear God's voice,
encounter Christ's presence
and be inspired to follow
where the Spirit leads.   AMEN.

ELIZABETH, ZECHARIAH AND JOHN THE BAPTIST

They were going to name him Zechariah after his father, but his mother said, 'No; he is to be called John.' They said to her, 'None of your relatives has this name.'

They began motioning to his father, to find out what name he wanted to give him. He asked for a writing tablet and wrote, 'His name is John.'

~ Luke 1:59–60 ~

Meditation

Expectations stand at every corner of a family's life:
the outside world tells them how to be 'perfect'
what and when and how much they should want
of every measured thing
of every unmeasurable thing
but family life is laced with the unexpected,
as newness is laced with fear,
families surprise each other
they surprise the world.

Prayer

Lord, not everyone is struck dumb by news of You,
or has a long longed for prayer answered
with an inexplicable miracle,
but every family has seen joy and disaster,
every family walks into their future
as blind as Zechariah was dumb.

Lord who are our Parent,
let us not be dumb to and for each other,
let us speak for ourselves
as Elizabeth did among her neighbours.
Let us speak up for each other as Zechariah did for his wife,
let us speak for what is right as John did for you, O God.
Let us stand, both alone and together,
for what we know to be right and true.   AMEN.

Suggested Readings

Luke 1:64–66   *Zechariah praises God*
Deuteronomy 6:6–7   *Keep the Faith*

Blessing

May I see the work of the Lord
in the unexpected things in life
and may the Lord unlock my tongue
from fear and doubt
to support and love and praise.

JAMES, JOHN AND ZEBEDEE

*When they had brought their boats to shore, they left everything and
followed him.*

~ Luke 5:11 ~

Meditation

We've given you all the love we could
and taught you all we know:
the teachings of our faith;
the wisdom of our years;
the values of our family;
the skills of our trade.

Now life is your teacher
and the world your classroom.
New adventures lie before you
and new horizons beckon you forth.

You may have left your nets,
but take the skills to earn yourself a living.
You may have left your home,
but take the faith and values that we've taught you.
You may have left your family,
but not the love in which we'll always hold you.

It is time to say 'Goodbye',
but instead let's say 'God be with you';
for in leaving
you leave something of yourself behind
and take something of home with you.

Prayer

Living God,
we praise You
for the call of Jesus to his first disciples
and for their proclamation of his resurrection
to the world.

Just as His word was alive for them,
let it be alive and active for us;
just as His call activated their belief,
let it inspire and activate our faith in You;
just as His love transformed their lives,
let it transform the values of our hearts.

Help us in our worship and our lives
to follow where You lead us,
to leave behind the things we cling to
and to discover
that we can hold far more in our hearts
than we can in our hands.

Help us to realize,
that made in Your image
and equipped with Your love,
we already have all that we need
to respond to Christ's call today.   AMEN.

Suggested Readings

       Luke 5:1–11   *Jesus calls the first disciples*
   Matthew 12:46–50   *The kindred of Jesus*

Blessing

May God bless
the people that shape us
and the values that make us.
The journeys we make
and the paths that we take.   AMEN.

SIMON AND HIS MOTHER-IN-LAW

After leaving the synagogue he entered Simon's house. Now Simon's mother-in-law was suffering from a high fever, and they asked him about her. Then he stood over her and rebuked the fever, and it left her. Immediately she got up and began to serve them.

~ Luke 4:38–39 ~

Meditation

Not quite my child,
but a child within the family,
the bearer of different customs
to the mix of our familiar traditions.
Your presence ripples
the once clear, still waters
of what we were
and I must share the care of what I love
while walking the fine line
that lies between interfering
and being helpful.

Not quite my mother,
but gifted the role of parent
in the bond of loving we share.
Tensions lie in the spaces
of our conversations
as we test the water
of who we are to each other.
Trust lies between us
that neither of us will hurt
or interfere in the relationship
we individually hold.

Not quite ... family
Not quite ... comfortable
Learning love.

Prayer

God of entwining relationships,
in the difference of opinions,
practice and tradition;
in the similarity of hopes,
life and love;
You weave the cords
that pull people together
with what is familiar
and then expand the length
to find room within the design
for variety that will strengthen
and grow experience.
In our encounters with those
who share our lives
may our love unite us;
our tension fire us;
and Your presence guide us.   AMEN.

Suggested Readings

Luke 4:38–44	*Jesus heals Simon's mother-in-law*
Ruth 1:11–22	*Ruth chooses to stay with her mother-in-law*

Blessing

May God's Spirit twine around my heart
that I may enjoy
that which draws people together
and investigate the spaces that lie between.   AMEN.

MARTHA AND HER SISTER MARY

Now as they went on their way, he entered a certain village, where a woman named Martha welcomed him into her home. She had a sister named Mary, who sat at the Lord's feet and listened to what he was saying. But Martha was distracted by her many tasks.

~ Luke 10:38–40 ~

Meditation

A thousand things are on my mind.
My to-do list will keep me busy for some time.
A week at least.
And, of course, I'm doing it all for them, because someone
    has to.
And it's usually me.
Keeping busy, that's my thing.
And caring for them all.
And putting myself last.
And never putting my feet up.
And never sitting still.

When I do, you see, the thoughts come;
they fill my head and disquiet my heart.
They haunt me. They rob me of sleep.
They won't let me rest.

Mary, my sister, she has peace.
She has no need to hide from Him,
our special Guest.
She has no need to stay in the kitchen,
out of His way.

He knows. I'm sure of that.
He knows I'm 'worried and distracted'.
But how can I sit at His feet when nothing
is hidden from Him?

I so long to be like her, like Mary,
completely at ease when He looks at me,

when He looks into me.
I so long to stop running and to sit with Him
and to hear Him speak His words of peace
into my life.

Prayer

Searching God,
Your presence troubles me.
The silence that surrounds You alarms me.
You leave me no place to hide,
no noisy place to stop Your voice from reaching my ears.

And yet, it is a relief to know that I
am fully known, inside and out.
It is restful to know that disguises won't work
before Your eyes.

Open my eyes, Lord, so that I can see
more clearly and recognize the clutter
that keeps me from coming to You.
Help me to give up my need for busyness
and to sit down at last, at Your feet,
alongside my sister,
content and ready to hear You speak – now …

Suggested Readings

> Luke 10:38–42 *A visit from Jesus*
> Psalm 131 *Quiet trust in God*

Blessing

May the silence of God surround me;
may the calm of the Spirit fill me;
may the peace of Christ uphold me,
this and every day. Amen.

THE DEVIL

*When the devil had finished every test, he departed from him until
an opportune time.*

~ Luke 4:13 ~

Meditation

You should have seen me
that day in the garden.
So easy.
Words have such power
when coiled in temptation.

You should have seen me
that day on the mountain.
So alluring.
I had it all to give away
but chose to save it for later.

You should have seen me
mingling among the faithful.
So effortless.
Money, reputation and self-protection
win over loyalty every time.

You should have seen me
back in the garden, up on the hill, among the crowd.
So satisfying.
Death taken like any man,
the blood and screams to prove it.

So where was I
when the blood coursed through living veins
and the screams turned to shouts of joy
when the world saw this was not just any man?
I was there.
In that death-shrouded tomb.
Down but not out.

Prayer

Lead us not into temptation
and deliver us from evil.
Lord, only You have the power to save us.
When we are attracted
by something other than our humility,
when we feel equipped
by something other than our weakness,
when we are lured
by something other than others' needs,
may we step from the tomb which keeps us from You.
And may You see us for what we can be.
In Jesus' name we pray.   AMEN.

Suggested Readings

Luke 4:1–13   *The temptation of Jesus*
I Peter 5:6–11   *Keep alert*

Blessing

Goodness is stronger than evil.
Love is stronger than hate.
Light is stronger than darkness.
Life is stronger than death.
Victory is ours through him who loves us.

Desmond Tutu

QUEEN OF SHEBA

When the Queen of Sheba had observed all the wisdom of Solomon
… there was no more spirit in her.

~ 1 Kings 10:4–5 ~

Meditation

Dripping jewels,
perspiring perfume,
oozing wealth
she comes
this Queen of the south,
flaunting her caravan of credentials.

Intrigued by his fame,
aroused by his power,
armed with hard questions,
she seeks
this first lady of Sheba
to know Solomon for herself.

Listening to his answers,
growing through his wisdom
bathing in his faithfulness
she understands
this throne of Sheba:
there are some things money can't buy.

Blessing God,
thanking Solomon,
rejoicing in justice and righteousness
she sets out once more
this woman of Sheba.
And there is a new Spirit within her.

Prayer

Gracious Lord,
in a world where
we hang on the words

of the rich, the powerful,
the famous and the glamorous,
lured by the noose of their lifestyles,
thank heavens
Your wisdom still breaks through
in those who have the right Spirit.
Precious pearls inspire us from the lips
of luminary world and faith leaders
whose teachings we treasure.

But most wise people are not celebrities.
So bless children wise beyond their years
and all the ordinary people
whose faithful discernment and knowledge
transforms the lives of family, friend and workmate.

And bless You, Holy Spirit
for all who reveal God's truth to us.   AMEN.

Suggested Readings

1 Kings 10:1–13   *Queen of Sheba visits Solomon*
Luke 11:29–32   *Jesus praises the wisdom-seeking
queen*

Blessing

Spirit of the living God,
fall afresh on me.
Take me, melt me,
mould me, fill me.
Spirit of the living God
fall afresh on me.

Daniel Iverson, CH4 *619*

HEROD AND HERODIAS

But Herod the ruler, who had been rebuked by him because of Herodias, his brother's wife and because of all the evil things that Herod had done, added to them all by shutting up John in prison.

~ Luke 3:19–20 ~

Meditation

But that's not where it stopped,
was it, Herod, with John in prison?
You were the king;
you had the power;
you had everything you wanted,
or – at least – you could get it.
Nothing and no-one could stop you,
not the law, not your conscience,
not John.

How did you feel,
the day after your birthday feast,
when you came to
and you remembered what you had done?

And you, Herodias,
were you at all disturbed?
Or did you feel you had been set free
from the burden of this outspoken man?

King Herod, Queen Herodias,
were you afraid?
Did you sense somehow
that John, this holy and righteous man,
spoke out to proclaim
the coming of the true King,
the King whose power was hidden,
to be shown only
in unspeakable acts of love?

Prayer

I survey my kingdom, God,
and I don't want you in it.
If I give you a hearing
through those who speak to me of
Your better way,
how can I go on?

My fear of losing control
overwhelms me and holds me in its grip.

Forgive me, Lord.
Help me to lay down my crown
and hand over my orb and sceptre to the One
who alone can truly handle them.

When I look at Him,
in His purple robe,
being mocked and maligned
for me,
I see at last
what great power there is
in weakness.
In His name I pray.   AMEN.

Suggested Readings

> 1 Samuel 8   *Israel demands a king*
> John 19:1–5   *Here is the man*

Blessing

May the King of kings
give you the courage to be weak;
may the Lord of lords
give you the will to be held;
may the Lamb of God
uphold you with His love,
this and every day.

PHARISEES

Woe to you Pharisees! For you love to have the seat of honour in the synagogues and to be greeted with respect in the market-places.

~ Luke 11:43 ~

Meditation

Lord, help me to see
the Pharisee in me:
that devotee to doctrine
and fanatic of the faith,
that part of me
which desires to be honoured,
and fears to be criticized;
that hungers for power and thirsts for praise;
that self-appointed, self-anointed,
idol to myself.

Lord, help me to see
the Pharisee in me:
that partisan for prayer
and follower of the faith,
that part of me
which desires to serve
and fears to be idle;
that hungers for justice and thirsts for peace;
that God-appointed, God-anointed,
image of your Love .

Prayer

Great God,
show me the humility
which recognizes its own arrogance,
realizes its own ignorance
and reveres only You.

A humility, which leads me to a faith:
that is not influenced by praise
nor blind to criticism;

that admits its mistakes
and recognizes its needs;
that is quick to affirm
and slow to criticize.

Fill my soul with Your Words of Love
that I may discover the strength
to serve both You and others
in my daily life.   AMEN.

Suggested Readings

Luke 18:9–4   *The Pharisee and the tax-collector*
Matthew 23:1–36   *Jesus denounces scribes and
Pharisees*

Blessing

Thus you shall bless the Israelites:
You shall say to them,
The LORD bless you and keep you;
the LORD make his face to shine upon you
    and be gracious to you;
the LORD lift up his countenance upon you
    and, give you peace.

Numbers 6:23b–26

LAWYERS

Woe to you lawyers! For you have taken away the key of knowledge; you did not enter yourselves and you hindered those who were entering.

~ Luke 11:52 ~

Meditation

Powerful words.
Scripture.
We need to keep it safe,
in the right hands,
locked away from harm.
Kept sterile.
Untainted.

The risk of infection
is too great in the wrong hands.
Mishandled.
Abused.
Fools.

Interpretation is the key.
Years of study,
pouring over every word.
Handling text
with kid gloves.

To do anything else
would be dangerous.
Explosive.
Cataclysmic.

They do not know what could happen.
I could not dare to
imagine.
I hold the keys.
I have been entrusted with them.

Locked.
Shut.
Silenced.

It is my job.
Woe is me ...

Prayer

Lord, we keep the door tight shut
from fear, misunderstanding and distrust
of others.
Free us from our power
and allow us to understand.
Open the door to new possibility
for Yours alone is the Kingdom.
There are no keys,
not any more.
And in Your love You always leave the door ajar.
That is who You are.
You love us.
May it be so.   AMEN.

Suggested Readings

Luke 11:37–54   *Foolishness of the Pharisees*
Ecclesiastes 1:12–18   *Knowledge and foolishness*

Blessing

Let the love of God
fill your hearts and minds.
Set yourself free
from what vexes you.
For God is with you
and God will bless you,
today and always.

MARY MAGDALENE, JOANNA, SUSANNA AND MANY OTHERS

As well as some women who had been cured of evil spirits and infirmities: Mary Magdalene, from whom seven demons had gone out, and Joanna, the wife of Herod's steward Chuza, and Susanna, and many others, who provided for them out of their resources.

~ Luke 8:2–3 ~

Meditation

Following Jesus, the women
liberated
to know their place.
They give according to their considerable means.

It costs to keep
the travelling God-show on the road.
Even disciples cannot live alone
by every word that proceeds
from the mouth of the Lord.
Daily bread,
baked by loving female hands
is broken in community.
Daily clothing,
a sacrament of sewing,
is washed and mended.
And when day is done,
the ministry of listening,
healing and caring
affirms and enables Jesus and His friends.

Praying and proclaiming together
power exchanged for empowerment,
riches for redemption,
the wealthy women add their voices
to the Kingdom choir.
Following Jesus – the women:
Mary Mag, Joanna, Susanna
and the many others ...
Lord, may what I give from my means

be enough for me to be counted
among the many others.

Prayer

Father and Mother God,
bless those who have wealth and influence
and use them for the greater good of all.
And bless those, rich and poor,
who use their inner resources and God-given talents
in the service of the Kingdom.

We give thanks for the ministry of women
from generation to generation
and ask blessing on women today,
ordained and lay,
who minister in myriad ways
in kirks[1] and kitchens,
homes and hospitals,
schools and social services,
boardrooms and bars.
But most of all, Lord,
thank You for team ministry –
the crucible of witness and mission,
the only true image of You on earth.   AMEN.

Suggested Readings

> Luke 8:1–3   *Women accompany Jesus*
> Luke 24:1–12   *Women witness to the resurrection*

Blessing

May God bless your purse.
May God bless your time.
May God bless your talents.
And may God gift you the means
to use them
according to His purpose.   AMEN.

---

[1] Kirk – a Scottish word for a 'church'.

JOSEPH OF ARIMATHEA

Now there was a good and righteous man named Joseph, who, though a member of the council, had not agreed to their plan and action. He came from the Jewish town of Arimathea and he was waiting expectantly for the kingdom of God.

~ Luke 23:50–51 ~

Meditation

The bully tries to triumph
by belittling the opposition.
Their opinion is the one heard loudest
over the chatter of the throng,
and in their self-belief of righteousness
they undermine the thoughts of others
until all will agree with them.
Gossips whisper
of the scandal in the village
as a good man
offers security to one
who would be cast aside.
Rumour merchants
crumble the walls of credibility
in case the threat
weakens the hold
of those who believe they hold the power.

Another with my name
stood against the undermining tones
of a community
and in a birth
recognized the potential for life
and took you to the heart of the family.
In my name I stand against the bully
and welcome you to this inner sanctuary of mine,
for in death of past patterns
the doors of possibility
are burst open.

Prayer

Forgiving Father,
when those of strong opinion
want to have their way,
it can be hard to speak up
and offer a different opinion.
Not wanting to be belittled
for what matters,
we find ourselves caught in decisions
that undermine the values of our lives.
Forgive me
for those times
when what I thought has lain hidden
and instead I have chosen to go with the flow
rather than trusting the words
Your Spirit stirs within.
Encourage me
to discover
that even the solitary voice
can stir others
to choose the path of Christ.   AMEN.

Suggested Readings

Luke 23:50–56   *Joseph of Arimathea asks for Jesus' body*
Matthew 1:19–21   *An angel offers Joseph advice*

Blessing

God of courage,
may I be blessed to know
that all opinions matter;
that little voices count;
and that even those who hold the strongest view
have fears that lie within.   AMEN.

BOAZ AND RUTH

And now, my daughter, do not be afraid, for I will do for you all that you ask, for all the assembly of my people know that you are a worthy woman.

~ Ruth 3:11 ~

Meditation

Love(making) can be fraught with complications.
Past lovers (and their mothers) will have shaped who we
    are today.
Community expectations about
who is worthy of our love
impinge on the choices we might make.
Obligations fleck the light of romance
as the picture of the future develops.

Love(making) should be simple,
for the Creator inspires
the building of relationships
where all are valued
for the experiences of life they bring
and the ambitions they encourage
in the other.

Prayer

In all our relationships
with others,
You, God of grace,
invite us to take brave steps.
In those we love,
You encourage us
to be daring
that the best of You might be demonstrated to the world.
In those we struggle to love,
there are new encounters to be found
that might enable us
to understand them more.
Yet the focus of Your love

is the well-being of all
who live within relationship
and so Your Spirit guides us
to acknowledge
that we too are loved and need to be loved.
Enable me to love myself
and hear the qualities that others see within
that inspire them
and speak of Christ's love.   AMEN.

Suggested Readings

Ruth 4:6–13   *Ruth humbles herself for Boaz*
John 4:15–25   *The Samaritan woman and Jesus*

Blessing

God of love,
may You embrace us
as we encounter others
and may our embraces speak of
Christ's living love
and His Spirit's concern for the world.   AMEN.

THE SHEPHERDS

… and all who heard it were amazed at what the shepherds told them.

~ Luke 2:18 ~

Meditation

There are none closer to the earth.
And so they are forever looking up
at the face of a jealous brother
harvesting revenge,
at the smile of a stubborn prophet
seeking a boy and finding a king,
at a star-shot midnight sky
glittering like angels' wings.

There are none more dependent on the earth.
Yet they are starved of promises,
now worn like the crook
which chafes their weary hands;
now dry like the soil
which slows their stumbling feet;
now vulnerable like a lost sheep,
spreading fear among the flock.

Until they look down
into the face of a child
and witness promise touch the earth
amidst the smells and splinters.

And in the light reflected from a star
they become leaders not of sheep but of people;
protectors not of flocks but of a precious gift;
followers not of their own fate but of the Kingdom's
    calling.

Prayer

You call yourself Shepherd, Lord.
For You too are put down by prejudice
and hungry for justice and love.

You call yourself Shepherd.
For You too face danger and denial
to sit with those on the edges.
You call yourself Shepherd
for with You every step is an adventure,
every new pasture lush with possibility.
With eyes fixed on You and hearts hankering after You,
may we call ourselves shepherds, Lord,
in the work of Your Kingdom.   AMEN.

Suggested Readings

Psalm 23   *The Lord is my Shepherd*
Luke 8:2–20   *The shepherds tell of the birth of Christ*

Blessing

Good Shepherd,
make us humble in Your presence
make us hungry in Your service
make us followers of Your promise
make us leaders of Your people
that all might be lifted up and fed.

THE HAEMORRHAGING WOMAN

She came up behind him and touched the fringe of his clothes and immediately her haemorrhage stopped.

~ Luke 8:43 ~

Meditation

What power possessed me
to expose myself,
in all the soil and shame
of womanhood
so long shunned and hidden,
as if I was worthy of attention?

What power possessed me
I will never know.
It was the lightest of touches
but it was as if I ripped the robe
from his body
and left him bare and broken.

Perhaps it was the camouflage
of the crowd
that dared me come nearer
than to any other man.
Perhaps it was the closeness
of his cloak
that drew the gentle brush of fingers
to its very edges.

The power that possessed me
and cleansed me at that moment
came not from my feeble flesh
but from the fringes of heaven.
And it was he who bled.
And it was I who lived again.

Prayer

We are so unworthy, Lord,
the only place we deserve to be
is beside You.
We are so brazen, Lord,
all that is left
is to bring our shame before You.
We are so unclean, Lord,
the only action open to us
is to reach out and touch You.

For we know that somewhere
in the midst of life's commotion
healing waits to be harnessed.

May we never be discreet, Lord,
in our expecting
in our asking
in our receiving.
And may You always be
within arm's reach of our need.   AMEN.

Suggested Readings

> Luke 8:43–48   *The haemorrhaging woman*
> Psalm 116   *Psalm of thanksgiving*

Blessing

May the power of
the living Christ
the healing Christ
the blessing Christ
the touching Christ
the broken Christ
the bleeding Christ
the saving Christ
and the Christ present
in all places and for all time
fill us and free us.   AMEN.

THE POOR WIDOW

He looked up and saw rich people putting their gifts into the treasury;
he also saw a poor widow put in two small copper coins. He said,
'Truly I tell you, this poor widow has put in more than all of them;
for all of them have contributed out of their abundance, but she out
of her poverty has put in all she had to live on.'

~ Luke 21:1–5 ~

Meditation

Day in,
day out.

She worked.
Constantly, bleedingly present, in each of her jobs.

Yet at the same time, she was also invisible
serving, cleaning, clearing the way for others.

And with such pride and temerity.

The most menial of tasks,
dull, dreary drudge
that nobody else wanted to do.

But she did it gladly, cheerfully.
Not for the money,
precious little there was to be made.

She worked because it worked for her.
The busyness of hard labour
kept her mind away.

From loss, anger, grief and regret.
The man she married all those years ago.
Betrothed and beguiled.

Sure, she had lots to give thanks to God for.
Her children, and their children.
For all the joy of life now,
when they all gathered round her.

Her heart, overflowing with joy, God-given joy …
But she would also never forget the heartbreak
of how he was not the man she thought he was.

The stony silence
at the table as he ate noisily.
And she knew that she would later
suffer the blows of his
disappointments and bitter defeat.

Nursing the wounds that would never heal.

And in that ill-at-ease peace
that was achieved in the aftermath of violence,
she thanked God for another day.

But that was so long ago.
she was a widow, now.
She was poor, but she was also so rich
– in ways she could never dare dream.

And with that, she made her offering to God.
Her all, everything she had.

Day in,
Day out.

Prayer

We pray for all who suffer from
the shackles of domestic abuse.
May we remember those we cannot possibly dare to
    imagine.
Bless those who struggle to be free.
And bless those who have broken free
May they know Your loving touch, O God.   AMEN.

Suggested Readings

> 1 Samuel 2:7–8   *God transforms people*
> Psalm 146   *Praising God in sorrow*

Blessing

Go in peace.
May God protect you.
May God show you the way.
May God unfold to you the riches of this day.
Giving peace to all that worries or hinders you.
Today and evermore.   AMEN.

ZACCHAEUS

All who saw it began to grumble and said, 'He has gone to be the guest of one who is a sinner.'

~ Luke 19:7 ~

Meditation

It's human nature
to make judgements about someone
before they have spoken
or had the opportunity to befriend.
People are placed in categories
depending on their age, their size,
their gender, their sexuality,
or their occupation.
We label them –
too small, too rich, too wise;
male or female;
tax-collector, Pharisee, lawyer, banker;
'sinner'.
Then they can be neatly packaged
into a metaphorical box
and placed upon the figurative shelf
where they can be ignored,
or castigated
for the image they present.

It's Christ's nature
to reach for the sealed box
of judgement
and look inside
to meet the whole person.
With wonder he demonstrates the gift
of generosity, kindness and love
that might enhance the life
of the community.

Prayer

Forgive me, Lord,
for those times
when I have judged someone
by their appearance or occupation.
Teach me the value
of what is hidden and unknown
that I might allow
the mystery of a human presence
to unfold
as I meet others.
Help me embrace
the presence of Christ
in the discovery
of another's gifts.   AMEN.

Suggested Readings

Luke 19:1–10   *Story of Zacchaeus*
1 Samuel 16:1–13   *The anointing of Samuel*

Blessing

As God accepts the whole of me,
may Christ inspire me to accept another,
and the Holy Spirit make me daring in my encounters.
AMEN.

THE MAN BEATEN UP ON THE ROAD TO JERICHO

Jesus replied, 'A man was going down from Jerusalem to Jericho, and fell into the hands of robbers, who stripped him, beat him, and went away, leaving him half dead.'

~ Luke 10:30 ~

Meditation

Broken bones and bruises time can heal,
but not the fears and shame that haunt my soul.
I am vulnerable:
a victim of violence,
a hostage to hate,
another casualty in the race of life.

Whatever happened to the man I once knew?
Proud and strong.
Not afraid of today
or what tomorrow might bring.
Where has he gone?

He is living in the shadows waiting to appear,
he is buried in the earth waiting to be reborn,
he is cocooned inside me waiting to transform
from victim to survivor,
from captivity to liberty,
from death to life.

I yearn to be me. I yearn to be free.

Prayer

Servant of Love
and Shepherd of Peace,
join to Your own suffering
the pains of all who have been hurt
in body, mind and spirit.

Salve the souls of those who fall by the wayside of life,
in busy streets and school yards.
Be balm for the bruises of those who suffer,
in the isolation of homes and hospital wards.
Caress the cuts of those who bear the scars of violence
in their hearts and minds.

And heal us of our own brokenness
that we might not pass them by.   AMEN.

Suggested Readings

> Luke 10:25–37   *Parable of the Good Samaritan*
> Psalm 13   *A prayer for help*

Blessing

God knows me by my name because God gives me life.
God calls me by my name because God seeks my company.
God cherishes my name because God loves me.

My name is ...
and I am precious in the eyes of God.   AMEN.

HIS SERVANT ISRAEL

You whom I took from the ends of the earth and called from its farthest corners, saying to you, 'You are my servant, I have chosen you and not cast you off.'

~ Isaiah 41:9 ~

Meditation

Israel, Israel –
God-named after Jacob,
who struggled with his Lord.
You have struggled too.

Israel, Israel –
God-chosen to be His own:
the collective singular servant.
You are called to be faithful.

Israel, Israel –
God-filled history writ large
in sacred texts of Scripture.
You have a story that's infamous.

Israel, Israel –
God-bound in loving covenant,
His laws set on tablets of stone.
You broke the rules.

Israel, Israel –
God-expected, to deliver righteous fruits
of loving mercy, justice and peace.
You have disappointed.

Israel, Israel –
God-promised ancestor of Jesus:
wrong doing and wrong done to.
God is with you, and also with us.

And we struggle too.

Prayer

Mercy-loving God,
if I am ever tempted to cast the first stone
because Your chosen servant
has, in my opinion,
been caught in an act of unfaithfulness,
then let me hear Jesus' voice say,
'Let you who is without sin ...'

For Israel's hallowed history
is a light to all the nations –
her triumphs and failures
serving to teach us still.
And I bow my head, God,
and imagine my nation's story told
as acts of faithfulness or unfaithfulness
to be Your servant.
History repeats itself ...

Forgive me, Lord, for judging.
Forgive the nations' shortcomings.
Forgive Your struggling servant church.
Forgive Your plural individual disciples.
Unite us in Your Spirit as
Jesus' collective singular body on earth.
Bless us, Lord.
Bless Your servant Israel.
There but for the grace ...

Suggested Readings

> Luke 1:54   *Reference in Magnificat*
> Isaiah 41:8–13   *God's promise to His servant, Israel*

Blessing

May God bless your struggles.
May Christ redeem your missed marks.
May the Holy Spirit guide your choices.
May the One who is love
make us one in His love.   AMEN.

JACOB

... son of Jacob, son of Isaac, son of Abraham, son of Terah, son of Nahor ...

~ Luke 3:34 ~

Meditation

How can I serve the Holy One?
How can I come before Him, after what
I have done?

From before I was born I was crooked,
out to lie and cheat
and take advantage, even of
my brother.
Out always to get the best
for myself,
with hardly a thought
for those around me.

A stolen blessing: the lodestar
over my life.
Afraid to cross the path of
the one I betrayed.
Afraid to come face to face with my twin.

Jacob, more than flawed,
you give me hope.
For there was that day
when you turned around
and you wrestled
and you came face to face
with God
and you were changed.

Now we read your name
among those of the ancestors of
the Christ,

in whom was found no deceit,
no sin, no flaw,
only love.

Prayer

Holy Lord,
I want to thank You for the Book,
for in its pages I discover
people not too different from me,
people who need to confess
their imperfections,
their mistakes,
their sins.
And You hear them
and welcome them
and give them dignity
with Your forgiveness.
I praise You, Lord,
for the hope of a new beginning,
in Jesus' name.   AMEN.

Suggested Readings

Genesis 32:22–33   *Jacob wrestles with God*
Genesis 49:29–33   *Death of Jacob*

Blessing

May you know the freedom
of God's mercy and love
as you come to meet Him
face to face.   AMEN.

ELIJAH

When Ahab saw Elijah, Ahab said to him, 'Is it you, you troubler of Israel?'

~ I Kings 18:17 ~

Meditation

In days of old,
in the days of Elijah,
rulers were troubled by
prophets' pronouncements.
The word of the Lord, from the lips
of His servants,
cut like a two-edged sword
and it was heard.
As they spoke, kings were ousted
or raised up
according to God's will,
and the people trembled.

Then, the Carpenter came,
quietly,
wholeheartedly in God's service.
Some heard him,
the One who was himself the Word
and they listened and understood:
Here is God's Servant,
consumed, like Elijah, with zeal
for God's house,
willing to give of himself
until all is spent.
His name: Emmanuel.
With his presence
and his love
he troubles the world.

Prayer

God,
zeal doesn't have a good press
these days.

It frightens and unsettles us to find folk
who are consumed with longing for You.
And yet, You ask us to be single-minded
in following Christ,
whose whole being
was directed towards You.
He is to be our example.
Lord, we need Your help
to find for ourselves
the way we should serve.
Show us how to love You
and the world and its people
with Your kind of love:
A love that sometimes troubles,
but always brings blessing
from You.
In Jesus' holy name we ask.   AMEN.

Suggested Readings

> 1 Kings 19   *Elijah meets God*
> Hebrews 1   *God speaks through His Son*

Blessing

Spirit of life and power,
revive us in this hour
and stir our hearts to praise with true devotion.
Fill us with heavenly fire
and every heart inspire,
that we may serve the world with your compassion.

Iain D. Cunningham, CH4 608

SOLOMON

Consider the lilies, how they grow: they neither toil nor spin; yet I tell you, even Solomon in all his glory was not clothed like one of these.

~ Luke 12:27 ~

Meditation

If the rich were to step out
in their finery
and fill their cupboards
with the freshest food
and be distracted daily,
deliberating details,
not even the littlest lily
would be impressed.

Work and worry,
stress and struggling,
need and nervousness
about tomorrow
is the stuff of slavery.

Asking,
seeking,
trusting,
believing
is enough
to be the stuff of servants.

And it doesn't take the wisdom of kings
to find, among the folly,
the stuff of faith.

Prayer

I worry about worrying, Lord,
yet it seems the right thing to do
when the cupboards of my soul are bare
and tomorrow looms
like a familiar yet unwelcome guest.

Teach me, Lord,
in my threadbare, fickle faith,
how to seek You as sustenance,
how to serve You in sureness
and how to ask for nothing
but what You know I need.
So be it.

Suggested Readings

Proverbs 2:1–8   *The call of wisdom*
Luke 12:22–28   *Don't worry about tomorrow*

Blessing

In all we don't have,
for all we don't need,
for what we don't seek,
for when we don't ask,
bless us, Lord,
and show us Your Kingdom.

MARY

Then Mary said, 'Here I am, the servant of the Lord; let it be with me according to your word.'

~ Luke 1:38a ~

Meditation

First – the light!
'Do not be afraid. You have been blessed by God.'
Listening in wonder and amazement,
to the promise that I would bear a son,
God's Son.
The impossible!
Yet in my heart I knew,
that God had chosen undeserving me
and I could not stop myself saying,
'Let it be done.'

And in that moment,
when I first held him in my arms,
I felt a love so piercing,
that I wanted to cry out.
But instead, I whispered,
'Let it be done.'

And over the years
the two-edged blessings of motherhood –
joy and sorrow, laughter and pain,
expectation and disappointment.
But in my heart I knew that my son
was doing what had to be done.

Much later – the dark!
'Father it is finished, into Your hands, I place my spirit.'
Listening in wonder and amazement
to the agony of my son fulfilling promise.

And in that moment,
when I could not hold him in my arms,
I felt a love so piercing,
that I wanted to cry out.
But instead I whispered,

'Let it be done.'
And it had been.

For every generation –
it had been done. Amen!

Prayer

Let it be, Lord.
Let Your love grow
within the depths of me
not because I am worthy
but because without You there
within my virgin space
my life is barren.

Let it be, Lord.
Let the womb of my heart
cherish and birth Christ Jesus
in thought, word and deed
that Your presence on earth
may be magnified
and my soul may rejoice.
Let it be, Lord.
Let all Your promises
to all the generations
of the poor and the powerless,
the hungry and the humble
be fulfilled
as women, men and children
become mothers
of Your Word.

Suggested Readings

Luke 1:26–38   *Mary is visited by the angel Gabriel*
Luke 1:46–55   *Mary's song of praise*

Blessing

May the Mighty One
do great things for you.
May you know His love and mercy.
And may you sing Mary's song
all of your days.   AMEN.

JESUS

And Jesus increased in wisdom and in years, and in divine and human favour.

~ Luke 2:52 ~

Meditation

Whispered in emptiness.
Spoken in space.
Shaped in darkness.
Declared in the streets.
Rumour become reality.
And the Word was out.

Making sense of prophets' claims.
Turning real an angel's promise.
Pouring joy into a young girl's pain.
Resurrecting an old man's hopes.
Joining up the jumbled phrases
of an incoherent world.
Talking itself into unspeakable places.
And the Word was alive.

And wise men listened.
In palaces,
in pastures,
in stables,
in temples,
as a baby became a child, became a man,
became Saviour of the world.
And the Word is with us.

Prayer

The Word was love
right from the start, Lord.
You dared all, You risked all, You gave all
so that we might hear it even once.
It stutters in the blink of the first wakening stars,
it hums in the glare of the desert heat;

it sings beside seashores
and shouts hallelujah in the hills.
May we be wise enough to hear You
and to heed You, Jesus,
in every place and generation.   AMEN.

Suggested Readings

> Luke 3:41–52   *Jesus in the temple*
> Ephesians 1:3–14   *Our inheritance through Christ*

Blessing

Jesus loves me! he will stay
close beside me all the way;
he will always be my friend,
and his love will never end.

Jesus loves me.

Anna Bartlett Warner CH4 *563*

THEOPHILUS

… most excellent Theophilus …

~ Luke 1:3 ~

Meditation

Most excellent Theophilus,
friend of God.
Friends know each other well.
Friends are not afraid to see each other
face to face.

But this, your friend,
is the Maker of the universe;
the living God, into whose hands
it may be better not to fall,
for that is such a fearful thing.

Be not afraid, most excellent Theophilus.
Be not afraid.
I'll show you the living God
in the face of Him who arrived among us
as one who is helpless,
who had to grow, like you and I,
who learnt to walk and talk and trust
and who began to comprehend,
step by step,
the way he must walk.

Most excellent Theophilus,
I can do no more than tell His story,
for you to hear, to read, to study,
and to meet your friend,
day after day.

His story is in your hands now, Theophilus,
entrusted to your care.
Those later-born, like you,
long to meet your Friend and mine,

to look into His face,
and see His grace
and comprehend His love.

Prayer

Gracious God, my loving friend,
how blessed I am to have inherited
the story of Your love
for all humankind.
How fortunate I am to stand
in that long line of people
who, from our hidden beginnings
to this day,
have felt the longing to know You.
Help me to love You, Lord,
with all my heart and soul
and mind and strength
and to love my neighbours enough
to tell them of You,
their truest friend.   AMEN.

Suggested Readings

> Exodus 33:7–11   *The tent of meeting*
> 1 Corinthians 13   *Love*

Blessing

May God let light shine out of darkness
into your heart,
to give you the light
of the knowledge of the glory of God
in the face of Jesus Christ.   AMEN.

THE ELEVEN DISCIPLES

That same hour they got up and returned to Jerusalem; and they found the eleven and their companions gathered together. They were saying, 'The Lord has risen indeed, and he has appeared to Simon!'

~ Luke 24:33–34 ~

Meditation

Safety in numbers.
The best course of action
for a motley crew of post-crucifixion
not-quite-there-yet resurrection people.

Once before they'd left behind
nets and ledgers, friends and families,
when words were fresh and welcome.
Now they hid behind closed doors,
an uneasy brotherhood,
those same words stale and uninvited.

Safety in numbers.
The best course of action
when people burst in with idle talk
of empty tombs and familiar faces on the journey.

Then it's time to leave again,
to wonder at a hillside encounter,
to edge a little closer to the whys and wherefores,
to reveal a new way of understanding
age-old prophecies and songs,
to want never to be safe again.

Prayer

They were only eleven and a few stragglers.
But the truth that led them
from their old lives,
from the prison of their fears,
from a shuttered room

to a mealtime miracle and a mammoth task
was enough.
God of the past and the present,
may that truth be enough to save me
from wanting to be safe in Your service.   AMEN.

Suggested Readings

Luke 24:28–35   *The disciples hear of the Emmaus*
encounter
Acts 1:12–14   *The disciples gather in Jerusalem*

Blessing

Bless me in my giving up
that I might receive.
Bless me in my giving in
that I might believe.
Bless me in my giving all
that all my life may bear witness
to my Maker's miracle.

CLEOPAS AND HIS COMPANION

When he was at the table with them, he took bread, blessed and broke it, and gave it to them. Then their eyes were opened, and they recognized him: and he vanished from their sight.

~ Luke 24:30–31 ~

Meditation

Hands spoke without words:
as they lay upon the tablecloth
while conversation continued
and food was shared;
as they stretched across the table
to lift and break the bread
while words of blessing were spoken;
as they accidentally touched skin
revealing his presence
while the bread was shared.

Hands spoke without words:
with age and gender revealing
in the lines and texture,
the wrinkles and colour;
with the kind of work seen
in the roughness of palms
and the scuffed, misshapen nails
of labour;
with the marks of pain
in the tender flesh.

Hands should speak without words:
for they can usher forth excitement,
or hold another in their pain and sorrow;
for they can clench in anger with the frustration of not
     knowing what to do,
or they can play their part in a revolution
that creates a moment of heavenly presence.

Prayer

God of simplicity,
it is so easy to forget
how important our hands can be
in sharing with others
the story of faith.
We like to complicate what we tell of You
with special words and rituals
that speak of Your uniqueness.
Yet You invite us to keep it simple.
For Your story is told
when we share food with another;
Your compassion is offered
when we take the hand of a stranger
and share their tears;
Your love is shared
when we find a space for others in our lives.
May we always be reminded
that when we can find no words to say
that You reveal Christ's presence
in the movements of our hands.   AMEN.

Suggested Readings

> Luke 24:13–35   *The Emmaus road*
> Acts 19:1–6   *Paul baptizes at Ephesus*

Blessing

May the love of God,
placed in my hands in Jesus' name,
pour forth from my palms
at the Spirit's prompting.   AMEN.

JAIRUS' DAUGHTER

But he took her by the hand and called out, 'Child, get up!' Her spirit
returned, and she got up at once. Then he directed them to give her
something to eat.

~ Luke 8:54–55 ~

Meditation

Alive within themselves,
but dead to the world.
Too young, too old, too sick, too poor …
for the world to recognize their potential.
They are the hollow human husks
on the spoil heap of humanity;
waiting to be recognized,
seeking to be reborn
back into life and possibility.

But for God,
Jeremiah was not too young to be a prophet;
Sarah, not too old to become a mother;
David, not too flawed to lead his people;
Zacchaeus, not too short to see new horizons;
And Saul, not too callous to change his heart.

For with God,
no child is too lost to be welcomed home;
no person too sick to be embraced;
no life too spoiled to be held dear;
no soul too dead to be full of promise.

And so let us embrace and cherish:
the divine spark that illumes each soul;
the divine love that cradles each heart;
the divine spirit that dwells in each person;
that all may have life
and life abundant.

Prayer

Take my hand, Lord Jesus;
You, who healed both the sick and the healthy
and lead me out of the cruel cycle of relativity
and narrow confines of my own selfishness,
into the wide open spaces of Your love.

Open my heart and challenge my values,
that I may learn to see others
through Your loving eyes.

Make me alive to Your Spirit,
that I may see the potential in every life,
grasp the possibility of every moment
and embrace the promise of every encounter.   AMEN.

Suggested Readings

Luke 8:40–56   *Jairus' daughter*
Mark 10:13–16   *Jesus blesses little children*

Blessing

God be in my head,
and in my understanding;
God be in my eyes,
and in my looking;
God be in my mouth,
and in my speaking;
God be in my heart,
and in my thinking;
God be at my end,
and at my departing.   AMEN.

Book of Hours 1514

THE LITTLE CHILD PLACED IN THE CENTRE

An argument arose among them as to which one of them was the greatest. But Jesus, aware of their inner thoughts, took a little child and put it by his side, and said to them, 'Whoever welcomes this child in my name welcomes me, and whoever welcomes me welcomes the one who sent me; for the least among all of you is the greatest.'

~ Luke 9:46–48 ~

Meditation

Harassed.
That's the only way I can describe how I feel.

I love my children, every one of them.
With a love that will never flicker.

But I can't begin to explain
how my expectations are unrealistic.
Or so I'm told.

Children should be seen and not heard.
That's how I was raised.
A pat on the head and a smile of condescension.

I was never going to be like that.
I would be different.
Bits of my life and pieces of me,
would blend into a model of parenting
that bordered on perfection.

But that was the problem.
I expected too much.

But imagine my horror when I saw Jesus
talking, laughing, teaching
and I had the kids in tow.

Look at how they are dressed today
and far from quiet.
They can be seen AND heard.
Every whisper between them
is amplified and echoes, doubling in decibels.

Or at least, that's what it seems like to me.

No one else seems bothered.
We'll just sit back here, out of the way.
We don't want to disturb him.
I cannot let them ruin the reverence of the moment.
Cannot. Will not.

Imagine then the sinking feeling as he motioned to her
and placed her at the centre.

I could not hear what he was saying from here
but it dawned upon me
that what had least importance mattered most.
That the greatest was the least
and the least, greatest.

And there she was, right beside him,
right where she belonged.

Thank you, Jesus,
for teaching me what matters most
and least.

Prayer

Thank you God, for seeing me,
beyond the child that I am.
Here, You place me at the centre,
and give me Your love.
And so here also, I place You at the centre,
and give You my love.

Suggested Readings

Deuteronomy 4:9   *From one generation to the next*
1 Peter 5:1–5   *The Elders*

Blessing

May the wide-armed welcome of God
be yours today.
May you no longer hide in the shadows
or the pew at the back.
May you bask in the blessing of God Almighty
who bids us all welcome.
Today and every day.   AMEN.

US

Then turning to the disciples, Jesus said to them privately, 'Blessed are the eyes that see what you see!'

~ Luke 10:23 ~

Meditation

See you – rich proud and powerful people!
See him – the humble beggar on the street!
See her – the lowly mum struggling with four kids!
See them – the ones still on the outside!
See me – with my good intentions and myopic sight!

See us,
all God's people!
See with the Spirit of Christ.
See the goodness, the love, the needs.
See the evil, the apathy, the greeds.

See Jesus in everyone.
See everyone in Jesus.
Now, there's a vision.

Us,
eyes blessed by Jesus,
sent out on our mission.
There's a lot more than seventy of us now.
Holy Spirit,
lead the way.

Prayer

Spirit-Giving Lord,
bless our discipleship.

Root our discipline in Jesus:
our receiving and learning,
our obeying and trusting,
our confessing and pardoning,
our imitating and reflecting.
and our abiding in Christ forever.

Route our mission in Jesus.
Empower us to take up our cross.
And when we get hung up
on how others should exercise
their call to discipleship and ministry
bless our eyes anew.
And keep us together in faith and in love –
this present generation of Your Spirit.   AMEN.

Suggested Readings

Luke 10:1–12 and 17–20   *Mission of the seventy-two*
Luke 10:21–23   *Jesus rejoices in the Holy Spirit*

Blessing

O wad some power
the gift tae gie us
to see ourselves
as ithers see us.

From 'To a Louse' by Robert Burns

O you have the power
the gift to give us
to see ourselves
as you do see us.
Bless how we see the world, Lord.
Bless how we see each other.
Bless how we see ourselves.
And then, Lord,
bless our getting on with it!   AMEN.

The Months

NEW BEGINNINGS

Prayer

New every morning is your love,
O Great Creator;
and each new day is packed with potential.

I face the future, not knowing
the mysteries and opportunities
that life will bring me,
or how I will respond to them.

Help me to be ready for whatever
each new moment brings:
if I am to speak, help me to speak wisely;
if I am to act, help me to act justly;
if I am to wait, help me to wait patiently.

May Your presence pervade the lives
of all those who face
new challenges,
new opportunities,
new life,
new endings,
and new beginnings
in the journey of life;
that they may know You walk beside them
today, tomorrow, and for ever more.   AMEN.

Prayer Activity

Look at the news each day for items or stories
that speak of new beginnings. These might be the
family announcement of a birth or a wedding; the
advertisement of a new job; or the start of a new
peace accord. Pray for one new beginning each day.
You may wish to keep a list or make a collage of these
and look back at all the new things you have prayed
for at the end of the month.

Classic Prayer

Be thou a bright flame before me,
Be thou a guiding star above me,
Be thou a smooth path below me,
Be thou a kindly shepherd behind me
Today, tonight and forever.

St Columba

LOVE

Prayer

Lord of love found in parenting
as words of encouragement are spoken;
or advice is offered;
or boundaries are set;
found in the childhood playfulness
as laughter lights the day;
or tears stain the pain;
or hugs remind another of importance.

We remember that not every home
or family enjoys healthy relationships
and pray for those who feel unwelcome in their families;
whose ties are stretched to breaking point;
for whom expressions of love cross personal boundaries.

Lord of love found in friendships
as interests are shared
and stories told;
as support in difficult times is given
and received;
as silence sounds with companionship.

We remember those
who find friendship hard
because they find it difficult to trust
or shyness holds them back.
Or those for whom friendship asks too much
and puts them at risk of breaking confidence in others
or the boundaries of the law.

Lord of love expressed in the most intimate of relationships,
as men and women find soul mates and lovers.

We remember those who have been abused in the name of
    love
and those who love too much.

Lord of unconditional love,
You ask us to love beyond our limits

and to include within our relationships
those we do not know
and those we do not understand or like.
May Your Spirit remind us
that even when we are unloveable You love us
    unconditionally.   AMEN.

Prayer Activity

In Greek there are four words for love (*eros* –
passionate love; *philia* – friendship; *storge* – familial
affection; *agape* – unconditional love), each offering a
different expression of the breadth of love. Individually
or as a group, create a 'Love' map. Place yourself/
family/group at the centre and then each day grow a
branch connecting to those we are passionate about,
those who are held as friends, those who are our family,
and those we struggle to love unconditionally. Start
with simple relationships, using them as a focus for
prayer in the first week, slowly extending and adding
over the month. Some people may appear in more
than one group.

Classic Prayer

Come, my Light, my Feast, my Strength:
such a Light, as shows a feast:
such a Feast, as mends in length:
such a Strength, as makes his guest.
Come, my Joy, my Love, my Heart:
such a Joy, as none can move:
such a Love, as none can part:
such a Heart, as joys in love.

George Herbert 1593–1633

LENT

Prayer

And lead us not into temptation, but deliver us from evil.

Gracious God, let us take time this Lent
to loosen ourselves from the complexities of life.
Just as You guided Jesus in the desert,
hold us true to You in all that tempts us
away from Your discipleship road.

May we pause to remember those
whose lives are dominated by temptation.
For those who suffer from addictions of drugs and alcohol.
For gamblers of money, time and lives
and for all who will lose as a consequence.
For the agony of the parent
who suspects a child to have an eating disorder.
For those whose lives are riddled with pain and anger
and a need to take revenge.

Lord Jesus, temptations of mind, body and spirit
are ours to contend with.
But You show us how to defeat them
in obedience and trust that is so perfect –
we cannot even begin to understand.
Teach us this Lent
to recognize all that distances ourselves from You
and in drawing closer to You,
may we look at others with fresh eyes
and the costly, forgiving love that is Yours and Yours alone.
Loosen us to Lent, that we loosen our grip on our fears,
that we may have hands free
to touch Your humility
to feel our humanity
to grasp what is possible but just out of reach.   AMEN.

Prayer Activity

Make this Lent an opportunity to encounter in prayer the struggles of people in their myriad forms.

Each day, find a story in the news of a person or a family or a group of people, and choose to pray for them. Don't be afraid to pray for those whom you have never prayed for before. If you want to be a little more active, create a collage of pictures from the news of people and subjects you are praying for.

Classic Prayer

Comfort, O merciful Father,
by thy Word and Holy Spirit,
all who are afflicted or distressed
and so turn their hearts unto thee,
that they may serve thee in truth
and bring forth fruit to thy glory.
Be thou, O Lord, their succor and defence,
through Jesus Christ our Lord.

Philip Melancthon 1497–1560

EASTERTIDE

Prayer

Lord, the opening of a tomb
was not a one-day wonder
for awe-struck women and wide-eyed men.
And death did not deceive us
to creep from a cold slab
and hang in the shadows
licking its wounds and waiting its turn.
You made sure of that,
just as we are sure You never left us
in the first place
but stayed, albeit quietly,
waiting to turn the world around.

With this in mind, Lord,
we pray this day and every day
for echoes of You in places where sin lurks,
for signs of You in places where nothing grows,
for Your presence in places in need of change.

With this in mind
we pray this day and every day
that the lost may sense Your footsteps,
that the fearful may stand firm in You,
that the lonely may recognize You.

With this in mind
we pray this day and every day
for cold hearts to be warmed,
for quiet courage to confront evil,
for life in all its fullness to fill us
and to set us free.

We pray for Eastertide,
for the turning of the tide,
for the love inside us
to grow and to go with You.   AMEN.

Classic Prayer

Thou hast renewed a right spirit within us.
Thou has turned again and we are quickened.
Even that which we have asked for –
we believe that we have it.
Really and truly we believe thy whole good news.
Behold us: thy people who now rejoice in thee.

From 'The Steepness of the Brae' by Revd George F. MacLeod [1]

---

[1] Revd George F. MacLeod, 'The Steepness of the Brae', *The Whole Earth
Shall Cry Glory*, Wild Goose Publications, 1985.

HOLY SPIRIT

Prayer

Welcome, Holy Spirit of God,
Longed-for at Your coming.
We need Your prompting to lead us into prayer.

Day after day after day
men and women go to work to make a living.
Help us remember
and not take for granted
those without whose effort we could not live;
those whose wages are a pittance,
too little to flourish,
too little to fulfil responsibilities;
those whose coffers are full,
and yet their hearts are empty
for they live only for themselves.

Day after day after day
in this our ill-divided world
men and women go hungry;
children suffer for lack of clean water.
Help us in our plenty to remember them;
help us to remember justice
and be among those who
speak for the voiceless;
help us give readily
of time, talent and money
to ease anguish on the earth.

Day after day after day
there are those who yearn for
a glimpse of the One
who provides bread from heaven
and the wine of gladness.
Help us remember that we live
not by bread alone
but by every word God speaks;
help us remember that
the hidden One is made present
in those who follow in His way;

help us reach out to those
who need His healing touch.

Day after day after day,
locked up in the upper room,
we wait for the flames to come
and for the fire to burn in us,
so we may have courage and strength
to let ourselves be guided by You,
Spirit of truth.
May our hearts be fertile ground
for the growing of love, joy, peace,
patience, kindness, generosity,
faithfulness, gentleness and self-control:
Your fruit in us.
Against such things there is no law.   AMEN.

Prayer Activity

Cut out feathers in different sizes from white paper and
glue them on a piece of cardboard in the shape of a bird.
(You might be able to find and collect real bird feathers
when you go for walks.) Do some each day. Before
you glue the feathers in place, you might want to write
underneath them (or on them) the names of people or
places you would pray for the Spirit to touch that day.

Classic Prayer

Spirit of God, with your holy breath
you cleanse the hearts and minds of your people;
you comfort them when they are in sorrow,
you lead them when they wander from the way,
you kindle them when they are cold,
you knit them together when they are at variance,
and you enrich them with your many and various gifts.
We beseech you daily to increase
those gifts which you have entrusted to us;
that with your light before us and within us
we may pass through this world
without stumbling and without straying.

Erasmus 1466–1536

GENERATIONS

Prayer

In the forgotten corner of the cupboard of our prayers
we come across photographs of every generation.
From sepia to technicolour to multi-million mega pixels
we hold in our hearts the memories we have
of the generations that have gone before us
and so we pray for our world in all its generations.

For the silent generation,
we remember the indelible impact of war,
we pray for children who endure the pain of warfare
and we pause to remember those
who still fight for civil rights.

With the baby boomers,
we celebrate the developments of technology,
We pray for the adventure of new discoveries
on earth and in space.
And we hold the struggle of counter-culture,
its lures and trappings.

Generation X calls us to pray for the pain of places
like Vietnam, both past and present.
That nations will learn to live with one another in peace
and the warheads of suspicion are made redundant.

Generation Y teaches us to pray for a fast-paced world
where information is everywhere.
May we see the clarity of God
amidst the clamour of media, of fear and distrust.
May terror cease in God's transforming love
and may we know that God still calls us to be His.

And we pray for today's generation,
the new silent Generation Z.
Global digitalization leaves no stone unturned.
May God teach us in this frenetic pace of today,
to listen for His still small voice of calm.

Lord God, these are our generations.
Teach us to find Your prophetic word and to hear Your truth
and speak of Your love, yesterday,
today and tomorrow. AMEN.

Prayer Activity

Take time to look through family photographs. Give thanks for the memories that come alive and trace through the stories that are told in these pictures. Each day, pick up a photograph and pray, for the people, the place and the situation within which the photo is taken. There might be something you have chosen to forget that you need to work through in prayer and you might see something that you have never noticed before. Feel free to write down your thoughts and offer this as your prayer.

Classic Prayer

Through all the changing scenes of life,
in trouble and in joy,
the praises of my God shall still
my heart and tongue employ.

Nabum Tate 1652–1715
and Nicholas Brady 1659–1726

HOLIDAYS

Prayer

Be with me, O God,
as I escape the shackles of my normal routine
and the demands of work/school/chores.
Help me to recharge my soul
as well as my body –
and to realize that a holiday from my work
is not a holiday from my life of faith.

Thank you for all those
who water the plants and collect the mail,
who look after family pets,
and carry the extra load at work,
so that I can take this time out to rest and play.

Give me the strength and patience to deal
with those moments:
when children get under my feet;
when parents say 'Go outside and play';
when work emails invade my privacy;
when others interrupt my plans for peace.

May my holidays be Holy Days –
days when I can rejoice and celebrate
the many blessings I have
with the people I love.
Days when I can refresh my spirit
as well as my body.
Days when I can grow closer to You
as I celebrate the gifts of life.

Refresh, too, the lives of all those
who will have no holidays this year:
those who have no work to rest from,
those too elderly or sick to travel,
and those for whom each day is a struggle to live.

And prepare me, O God,
for my return to the rhythm and routine
of the chores/work that await me.   AMEN.

Prayer Activity

Pray for family members, friends and neighbours who
are away on holiday. Ask them to send you postcards
from the places or countries they visit. Put the postcards
somewhere that all those in your house can see them.
Find out what you can about each place/country and
include them in your daily prayers.

Classic Prayer

Lord, make our hearts places of peace
And our minds harbours of tranquillity.
Sow in our souls true love for you
And for one another;
And root deeply within us
Friendship and unity;
And concord with reverence,
So that we may give peace to each other sincerely
And receive it beautifully.

American Indian Traditional

FESTIVALS

Prayer

You enjoyed a celebration, Lord.
At the wedding of neighbours,
at the tables of the famous,
in the bustling streets of the city,
in an upstairs room with friends,
on a beach with faithful followers.

The laughter and song,
the chatter and cheer,
the party atmosphere,
the wine and bread,
the joyful reunions
a part of who You were
and what You promised us.

And so, in this month of festivals,
when communities, towns, cities and countries
celebrate culture, history, tradition and life,
we pray for all those
who share time and talents
through music, song, dance, theatre and the arts.

We pray for their laughter to infect us,
their creativity to inspire us,
and their ideas to motivate us.
We pray for safe journeys
for those who travel from far and near
to enjoy the gifts of others.
We pray for colour and comedy,
fanfare and frivolity,
fresh discovery and wisdom.

You enjoyed a celebration, Lord.
Celebrate with us the festivals of our lives
that we may sense Your presence
amidst the fun and freedom
and know Your invitation awaits us.   AMEN.

Classic Prayer

How grateful we are that in the perpetual mystery
You are walking and speaking with us now ...
and what You are Lord of is a dance and not a dirge ...
so that we too can dance wherever we may be.

From 'Lord of the Dance' by Revd George F. MacLeod [1]

---

[1] Revd George F. MacLeod, 'Lord of the Dance', *The Whole Earth Shall
Cry Glory*, Wild Goose Publications, 1985.

LEARNING

Prayer

As the new terms start for school children
and young people prepare
for college and university
it would be easy to believe
that education and learning
is the privilege of youth.
Yet in faith and life,
the Spirit of God
issues an invitation of wonder to all.
The world around is full of new experiences
for each of us to try
or watch others take pleasure in.
What we know is to be shared
that we might help others know more
or grow in our own understanding
from the passion of another.

As this new term starts,
God of wonder,
may we remember the youthful thirst for knowledge,
in sponge-like brains
that soak up all they hear and experience.
May their imaginations be sparked
by teachers who thrive on the sharing
of what they know.
When the classroom does not appeal,
help us to find new ways
to share knowledge.
In our later years
encourage us to be open to what is new
and willing to expand our experiences
so that we continue
to wonder at God's glory
shown in creation.   AMEN.

Prayer Activity

As an individual, family or group take up a new activity. Not all new things have to cost money. Why not learn a new walk in a different area – reading a map and encountering new obstacles and views; or visit an historic property and find out more about the people who occupied it. See this as an opportunity not just to learn something new, but to learn something about the others you share life with.

Classic Prayer

Teach us, good Lord,
to serve thee as thou deservest;
to give and not count the cost;
to fight and not heed the wounds;
to toil and not seek for the rest;
to labour and not ask for any reward
save that knowing we do thy will.

Ignatius of Loyola 1491–1556

HARVEST

Prayer

The light is lessening in these days,
Lord God, our Creator,
and yet this is the season of
every colour and hue
of nature's palette,
displayed to the world
in the abundance of Autumn,
of harvest, of the fruits of the earth.
This is the season in which
you lavish on us,
in Your generosity,
so much more than we deserve.

Forgive us when we refuse to see
in everything around us
Your love and care
for all Your children.
Forgive us when we refuse to share
Your gifts for living
with our sisters and brothers everywhere.
Forgive us our carelessness
with planet earth,
which You entrusted into our hands.

And so, at this time of plentiful providing,
we pray for those whose harvest
has failed and who therefore
go hungry again.
We pray that new ways be found
for all to share in the earth's goodness,
so that they may eat and be satisfied.

And so, at this time of growing darkness,
we pray for those who long for light,
who face deep sadness and sorrow,
who know stark loneliness and loss,
who struggle with disquieting thoughts.

We pray that they may find
in the Lord Jesus the peace they crave,
for He is the Light of the world,
and the Prince of Peace.

And so, at this time of thanksgiving,
we bless You, Lord God,
that You never weary in Your patience,
that You never leave us or forsake us,
that we can always place our trust in You.
We pray that You will keep us faithful
as we walk into the valley of fear and of
the threatening shadows of this time of year.
May Your presence guide and comfort us
until we see again
the dawn of the new day.
In Jesus' name we ask.   AMEN.

Prayer Activity

To appreciate the fruit of the earth, try eating a kind of
fruit or vegetable you have never tasted before. You
might have to learn how to prepare them.

Explore where these new fruits and vegetables come
from. Make a list of the countries, and find out as much
as you can about how the people there live.

Classic Prayer

Thou mastering me,
God! giver of breath and bread;
World's strand, sway of the sea;
Lord of living and dead;
Thou hast bound bones and veins in me,
    fastened me flesh,
And after it almost unmade, what with dread,
Thy doing: and dost thou touch me afresh?
Over again I feel thy finger and find thee.

Gerard Manley Hopkins 1844–89

REMEMBRANCE

Prayer

O God, our Help in ages past ...

In this season when we remember the
saints and souls,
heroes and heroines,
who have shaped our world
and moulded our lives;
we give thanks for all those
who have played their part in shaping
us into the people we are today.

We give thanks for
the loved ones who shaped our hearts,
the teachers who moulded our minds,
the friends who influenced our values
and the ones who first shared with us
the Good News of Your love for us.

We remember with real gratitude
all those who gave us their wisdom,
all those who gave us their love,
all those who gave us their time
and those who gave of themselves.
That we might have the freedom
to live as we do today.

O God, our hope for years to come ...

May we find the same strength of character
to share the legacies of love,
the wisdom of age
and the values of our faith,
that will help shape the lives of others.

May we find the same strength of faith
to stand up
for what we believe in,

for the freedom of others
and for the rights of the oppressed.
That we too will take our place among
the honour roll of Your saints
on earth and in heaven.   AMEN.

Prayer Activity

Create a collage of pictures and/or a list of names of
the people, places and events that have shaped your
life. Add a new one to the list each day and include
them in your prayers.

Classic Prayer

Almighty God from whom all thoughts of truth and peace
   proceed:
kindle, we pray you, in the hearts of all people
the true love of peace;
and guide with your pure and peaceable wisdom
those who take counsel for the nations of the earth;
that in tranquillity your kingdom may go forward,
till the earth be filled with the knowledge of your love:
Through Jesus Christ our Lord.

Francis Paget 1851–1911

EDGES AND EXTREMES

Prayer

We pray for the extremes of December.

In its dawning,
red ribbons remind us that
this is World Aids Day.
And united we stand
in our fight against HIV.

Sterling stars show the places
where the rich can spend in excess
while the poorer flirt with debt.
And as cards give instant credit
street beggars ask for change.

Greetings, gifts, journeys and meals!
Children excite while parents stress
and some folk are quite exhausted.
And there seem so many deadlines
before we celebrate God's lifeline.

From Christmas Day to Auld Lang Syne –
death and loss and loneliness
bite deeper at this time of year.
And quiet cups of kindness
brew auld acquaintance not forgot.

A month of cherished family and friends
or a time when relational tensions
will be brought to breaking point.
And love or lack of it
gets to us all at this time of year.

We pray for the extremes of December –
extremes of age and situation and poverty.
For You, God, understand extremes.
Coming to earth as a poor and helpless baby?
Take our faith to the extremes, Lord,
for that's where Christ's enfleshed.   AMEN.

Classic Prayer

Loving God, help us remember the birth of Jesus,
that we may share in the song of the angels,
the gladness of the shepherds,
and worship of the wise men.

Close the door of hate
and open the door of love all over the world.
Let kindness come with every gift and good desires with
    every greeting.
Deliver us from evil by the blessing which Christ brings
and teach us to be merry with clear hearts.

May the Christmas morning make us happy to be thy
    children,
and Christmas evening bring us to our beds with grateful
    thoughts,
    forgiving and forgiven, for Jesus' sake.   AMEN.

Robert Louis Stevenson 1850–94

Using *Pray Now 2013*
as a Worship Resource

Below is an example of how to take a day of *Pray Now* and augment it to produce a shorter act of communal worship. Essentially all the sections can be used or just the leader's introduction followed by the Bible reading, the meditation, a short silence, the prayer and the blessing – this may be all that is required for opening devotions.

The service may be led by one voice but has opportunity for several voices. Although the sections are read, the group may appreciate having individual copies of *Pray Now* to use during the service or to take away with them.

Day 31

Disciples – 'Us'

Leader   In our worship we will focus on today's generation of disciples – us! We begin by listening to a reading from St Luke Chapter 10 verses 17–23. The seventy missionaries return. Jesus rejoices in the vision that his disciples have been given and then he blesses them.

Reading   Luke 10:17–23 (*Luke 10:1–12 may be read first if longer reading is desired*)

Song   'I the Lord of sea and sky' *(CH4 251 music and words by Daniel L. Schutte)*

OR

'Sent by the Lord am I' *(Central American folk melody arranged by John Bell with words by Jorge Maldonado)*

Leader   'Then turning to the disciples, Jesus said to them privately, "Blessed are the eyes that see what you see!"' (Luke 10:23)

Are we blessed in our vision of others and of the world around us?

What a privilege to see with Christ-blessed eyes.

Listen now to this short meditation.

There will be a short silence afterwards for our own thoughts.

Meditation

See you – rich, proud and powerful people!
See him – the humble beggar on the street!
See her – the lowly mum struggling with four kids!
See them – the ones still on the outside!
See me – with my good intentions and myopic sight!

See us,
all God's people!
See with the Spirit of Christ.
See the goodness, the love, the needs.
See the evil, the apathy, the greeds.

See Jesus in everyone.
See everyone in Jesus.
Now, there's a vision.

Us,
eyes blessed by Jesus,
sent out on our mission.
There's a lot more than seventy of us now.
Holy Spirit,
lead the way.

Silence (optional)

Reflection (optional)

Leader   What came out of that meditation for you?

Does anyone want to share their thoughts?

OR

Who are the rich, proud and powerful of today?

How can we influence them?

Are there 'humble beggars' in our own community?

How can we help and enable those who are poorest?

Is there anything that this church could do to assist double or single parents who are struggling?

Who are the ones on the outside today?

Does the church welcome those who are marginalized?

Is it possible to see Jesus in everyone?

(*You will wish to select a few questions.*)

Prayer

Spirit-Giving Lord,
bless our discipleship.

Root our discipline in Jesus:
our receiving and learning,
our obeying and trusting,
our confessing and pardoning,
our imitating and reflecting.
and our abiding in Christ forever.

Route our mission in Jesus.
Empower us to take up our cross.
And when we get hung up
on how others should exercise
their call to discipleship and ministry
bless our eyes anew
and keep us together in faith and in love –
this present generation of Your Spirit.   AMEN.

(*There is a place here if desired for additional extempore prayers of thanksgiving and intercession.*)

Blessing

CH4 620 (*music David Iverson, words Michael Baughen*)
(NB this may be spoken by the leader, or another, or said together, or sung together.)

Spirit of the living God,
move among us all;

make us one in heart and mind,
make us one in love,
humble, caring,
selfless, sharing.
Spirit of the living God,
fill our lives with love.

Additional Resources

'The Church is wherever God's people are praising' (*CH4* 522).

'Will you come and follow me' (*CH4* 533).

'May the mind of Christ my Saviour' (*CH4* 536).

'When I needed a neighbour' (*CH4* 544 – good for all-age worship).

'When we are living in the Lord' (*CH4* 726).

Pray Now 2013 Daily Lectionary

Sunday 2 December

Jeremiah 33:14–16
Psalm 25:1–9
1 Thessalonians 3:9–end
Luke 21:25–36

Monday 3 December

Isaiah 2:1–5
Psalm 122
Matthew 8:5–11

Tuesday 4 December

Isaiah 11:1–10
Psalm 72:1–4, 18–19
Luke 10:21–24

Wednesday 5 December

Isaiah 25:6–10*a*
Psalm 23
Matthew 15:29–37

Thursday 6 December

Isaiah 26:1–6
Psalm 118:18–27*a*
Matthew 7:21, 24–27

Friday 7 December

Isaiah 29:17–end
Psalm 27:1–4, 16–17
Matthew 9:27–31

Saturday 8 December

Isaiah 30:19–21, 23–26
Psalm 146:4–9
Matthew 9:35 — 10:1, 6–8

Sunday 9 December

Malachi 3:1–4
Philippians 1:3–11
Luke 3:1–6

Monday 10 December

Isaiah 35
Psalm 85:7–end
Luke 5:17–26
1 Thessalonians 1

Tuesday 11 December

Isaiah 40:1–11
Psalm 96:1, 10–end
Matthew 18:12–14
1 Thessalonians 2:1–12

Wednesday 12 December

Isaiah 40:25–end
Psalm 62
Matthew 11:28–end
1 Thessalonians 2:13–end

Thursday 13 December

Isaiah 41:13–20
Psalm 145:1, 8–13
Matthew 11:11–15
1 Thessalonians 3

Friday 14 December

Isaiah 48:17–19
Psalm 1
Matthew 11:16–19
1 Thessalonians 4:1–12

Saturday 15 December

2 Kings 2:9–12
Psalm 80:1–4, 18–19
Matthew 17:10–13
1 Thessalonians 4:13–end

Sunday 16 December

Zephaniah 3:14–end
Isaiah 12:2–end
Philippians 4:4–7
Luke 3:7–18

Monday 17 December

Genesis 49:2, 8–10
Psalm 72, 1–5, 18–19
Matthew 1:1–17
1 Thessalonians 5:12–end

Tuesday 18 December

Jeremiah 23:5–8
Psalm 72:1–2, 12–13, 18–end
Matthew 1:18–24
1 Thessalonians 5:12–end

Wednesday 19 December

Judges 13:2–7, 24–end
Psalm 71:3–8
Luke 1:5–25
2 Thessalonians

Thursday 20 December

Isaiah 7:10–14
Psalm 24:1–6
Luke 1:26–38
2 Thessalonians 2

Friday 21 December

Zephaniah 3:14–18
Psalm 33:1–4, 11–12, 20–end
Luke 1:39–45
2 Thessalonians 3

Saturday 22 December

1 Samuel 1:24–end
Psalm 113
Luke 1:46–56

Sunday 23 December

Micah 5:2–5a
Magnificat
Hebrews 10:5–10
Luke 1:39–45 [46–55]

Monday 24 December

2 Samuel 7:1–5, 8–11, 16
Psalm 89:2, 19–27
Acts 13:16–26
Luke 1:67–79

Tuesday 25 December

Isaiah 52:7–10
Psalm 98
Hebrews 1:1–4 [5–12]
John 1:1–14

Wednesday 26 December

2 Chronicles 24:20–22
Psalm 119.161–168
Matthew 10:17–22
Psalm 13

Thursday 27 December

Exodus 33:7–11a
Psalm 117
1 John 1
John 21:19b–end

Friday 28 December

Jeremiah 31:15–17
Psalm 124
1 Corinthians 1:26–29
Matthew 2:13–18

Saturday 29 December

1 John 2:3–11
Psalm 96:1–4
Luke 2:22–35

Sunday 30 December

1 Samuel 2:18–20, 26
Psalm 148 [or 148:7–end]
Colossians 3:12–17
Luke 2:41–end

Monday 31 December

1 John 2:18–21
Psalm 96:1, 11–end
John 1:1–18

Tuesday 1 January

Numbers 6:22–end
Psalm 8
Galatians 4:4–7
Luke 2:15–21

Wednesday 2 January

1 John 2:22–28
Psalm 98:1–4
John 1:19–28

Thursday 3 January

1 John 2:29 — 3:6
Psalm 98:2–7
John 1:29–34

Friday 4 January

1 John 3:7–10
Psalm 98:1, 8–end
John 1:35–42

Saturday 5 January

1 John 3:11–21
Psalm 100
John 1:43–end

Sunday 6 January

Isaiah 60:1–6
Psalm 72:[1–9]10–15
Jeremiah 31:7–14
Matthew 2:1–12

Monday 7 January
John 3:22—4:6
Psalm 2:7–end
Matthew 4:12–17, 23–end

Tuesday 8 January
1 John 4:7–10
Psalm 72:1–8
Mark 6:34–44

Wednesday 9 January
1 John 4:11–18
Psalm 72:1, 10–13
Mark 6:45–52

Thursday 10 January
1 John 4:19–5:4
Psalm 72:1, 17–end
Luke 4:14–22

Friday 11 January
1 John 5:5–13
Psalm 147:13–end
Luke 5:12–16

Saturday 12 January
1 John 5:14–end
Psalm 149:1–5
John 3:22–30

Sunday 13 January
Isaiah 43:1–7
Psalm 29
Acts 8:14–17
Luke 3:15–17, 21–22

Monday 14 January
Hebrews 1:1–6
Psalm 97:1–2, 6–10
Mark 1:14–20

Tuesday 15 January
Hebrews 2:5–12
Psalm 8
Mark 1:21–28

Wednesday 16 January
Hebrews 2:14–end
Psalm 105:1–9
Mark 1:29–39

Thursday 17 January
Hebrews 3:7–14
Mark 1:40–end
Psalm 21

Friday 18 January
Hebrews 4:1–5, 11
Psalm 78:3–8
Mark 2:1–12

Saturday 19 January
Hebrews 4:12–16
Psalm 19:7–end
Mark 2:13–17

Sunday 20 January
Isaiah 62:1–5
Psalm 36:5–10
1 Corinthians 12:1–11
John 2:1–11

Monday 21 January
Hebrews 5:1–10
Psalm 110:1–4
Mark 2:18–22

Tuesday 22 January
Hebrews 6:10 end
Psalm 111
Mark 2:23–end

Wednesday 23 January
Hebrews 7:1–3, 15–17
Psalm 110:1–4
Mark 3:1–6

Thursday 24 January
Hebrews 7:25—8:6
Psalm 40:7–10, 17–end
Mark 3:7–12

Friday 25 January
Jeremiah 1:4–10
Psalm 67
Acts 9:1–22
Matthew 19:27–end

Saturday 26 January
Hebrews 9:2–3, 11–14
Psalm 47:1–8
Mark 3:20–21

Sunday 27 January

Nehemiah 8:1–3, 5–6, 8–10
Psalm 19 [*or* 19:1–6]
1 Corinthians 12:12–31*a*
Luke 4:14–21

Monday 28 January

Hebrews 9:15, 24–end
Psalm 98:1–7
Mark 3:22–30

Tuesday 29 January

Hebrews 10:1–10
Psalm 40:1–4, 7–10
Mark 3:31–35

Wednesday 30 January

Hebrews 10:11–18
Psalm 110:1–4
Mark 4:1–20

Thursday 31 January

Hebrews 10:19–25
Psalm 24:1–6
Mark 4:21–25

Friday 1 February

Hebrews 10:32–39
Psalm 37:3–6, 40–end
Mark 4:26–34

Saturday 2 February

Malachi 3:1–5
Psalm 24:[1–6] 7–end
Hebrews 2:14–end
Luke 2:22–40

Sunday 3 February

Malachi 3:1–5
Psalm 24:[1–6] 7–end
Hebrews 2:14–end
Luke 2:22–40

Monday 4 February

Hebrews 11:32–end
Psalm 31:19–end
Mark 5:1–20

Tuesday 5 February

Hebrews 12:1–4
Psalm 22:25*b*–end
Mark 5:21–43

Wednesday 6 February

Hebrews 12:4–7, 11–15
Psalm 103:1–2, 13–18
Mark 6:1–6

Thursday 7 February

Hebrews 12:18–19, 21–24
Psalm 48:1–3, 8–10
Mark 6:7–13

Friday 8 February

Hebrews 13:1–8
Psalm 27:1–6, 9–12
Mark 6:14–29

Saturday 9 February

Hebrews 13:15–17, 20–21
Psalm 23
Mark 6:30–34

Sunday 10 February

Exodus 34:29–end
Psalm 99
2 Corinthians 3:12—4:2
Luke 9:28–36 [37–43*a*]

Monday 11 February

Genesis 1:1–19
Psalm 104:1, 2, 6–13, 26
Mark 6:53–end

Tuesday 12 February

Genesis 1:20—2:4*a*
Psalm 8
Mark 7:1–13

Wednesday 13 February

Joel 2:1–2, 12–17
Psalm 51:1–18
2 Corinthians 5:20*b*—6:10
Matthew 6:1–6, 16–21

Thursday 14 February

Deuteronomy 30:15–end
Psalm 1
Luke 9:22–25

Friday 15 February

Isaiah 58:1–9*a*
Psalm 51:1–5, 17–18
Matthew 9:14–15

Saturday 16 February
Isaiah 58:9b–end
Psalm 86:1–7
Luke 5:27–32

Sunday 17 February
Deuteronomy 26:1–11
Psalm 91:1–2, 9–end [or 91:1–11]
Romans 10:8b–13
Luke 4:1–13

Monday 18 February
Leviticus 19:1–2, 11–18
Psalm 19:7–end
Matthew 25:31–end

Tuesday 19 February
Isaiah 55:10–11
Psalm 34:4–6, 21–22
Matthew 6:7–15

Wednesday 20 February
Jonah 3
Psalm 51:1–5, 17–18
Luke 11:29–32

Thursday 21 February
Esther 14:1–5, 12 –14
or Isaiah 55:6–9
Psalm 138
Matthew 7:7–12

Friday 22 February
Ezekiel 18:21–28
Psalm 130
Matthew 5:20–26

Saturday 23 February
Deuteronomy 26:16–end
Psalm 119:1–8
Matthew 5:43–end

Sunday 24 February
Genesis 15:1–12, 17–18
Psalm 27
Philippians 3:17 – 4:1
Luke 13:31–end

Monday 25 February
Daniel 9:4–10
Psalm 79:8–9, 12, 14
Luke 6:36–38

Tuesday 26 February
Isaiah 1:10, 16–20
Psalm 50:8, 16–end
Matthew 23:1–12

Wednesday 27 February
Jeremiah 18:18–20
Psalm 31:4–5, 14–18
Matthew 20:17–28

Thursday 28 February
Jeremiah 17:5–10
Psalm 1
Luke 16:19–end

Friday 1 March
Genesis 37:3–4, 12–13, 17–28
Psalm 105:16–22
Matthew 21:33–43, 45–46

Saturday 2 March
Micah 7:14–15, 18–20
Psalm 103:1–4, 9–12
Luke 15:1–3, 11–end

Sunday 3 March
Isaiah 55:1–9
Psalm 63:1–9
1 Corinthians 10:1–13
Luke 13:1–9

Monday 4 March
2 Kings 5:1–1
Psalms 42:1–2
Luke 4:24–30
Psalms 43:1–4

Tuesday 5 March
Daniel 2:20–23
Psalm 25:3–10
Matthew 18:21–end

Wednesday 6 March
Deuteronomy 4:1, 5–9
Psalm 147:13–end
Matthew 5:17–19

Thursday 7 March
Jeremiah 7:23–28
Psalm 95:1–2, 6–end
Luke 11:14–23

Friday 8 March

Hosea 14
Psalm 81:6–10, 13, 16
Mark 12:28–34

Saturday 9 March

Hosea 5:15—6:6
Psalm 51:1–2, 17–end
Luke 18:9–14

Sunday 10 March

Joshua 5:9–12
Psalm 32
2 Corinthians 5:16–end
Luke 15:1–3, 11b–end

Monday 11 March

Isaiah 65:17–21
Psalm 30:1–5, 8, 11–end
John 4:43–end

Tuesday 12 March

Ezekiel 47:1–9, 12
Psalm 46:1–8
John 5:1–3, 5–16

Wednesday 13 March

Isaiah 49:8–15
Psalm 145:8–18
John 5:17–30

Thursday 14 March

Exodus 32:7–14
Psalm 106:19–23
John 5:31–end

Friday 15 March

Jeremiah 26:8–11
Psalm 34:15–end
John 7:1–2, 10, 25–30

Saturday 16 March

Jeremiah 11.18–20
Psalm 7:1–2, 8–10
John 7:40–52

Sunday 17 March

Isaiah 43:16–21
Psalm 126
Philippians 3:4b–14
John 12:1–8

Monday 18 March

Joshua 2:1–14
Psalm 23
John 8:1–11

Tuesday 19 March

2 Samuel 7:4–16
Psalm 89:26–36
Romans 4:13–18
Matthew 1:18–end

Wednesday 20 March

Daniel 3:14–20, 24–25, 28
John 8:31–42

Thursday 21 March

Genesis 17:3–9
Psalm 105:4–9
John 8:51–end

Friday 22 March

Jeremiah 20:10–13
Psalm 18:1–6
John 10:31–end

Saturday 23 March

Ezekiel 37:21–end
Jeremiah 31:10–13
Psalm 121
John 11:45–end

Sunday 24 March

Luke 19:28–40
Psalm 118:1–2, 19–end
Isaiah 50:4–9a
Psalm 31:9–16 (*or* 31:9–18)
Philippians 2:5–11
Luke 22:14—end of 23

Monday 25 March

Isaiah 42:1–9
Psalm 36:5–11
Hebrews 9:11–15
John 12:1–11

Tuesday 26 March

Isaiah 49:1–7
Psalm 71:1–14 [*or* 71:1–8]
1 Corinthians 1:18–31
John 12:20–36

Wednesday 27 March

Isaiah 50:4–9a
Psalm 70
Hebrews 12:1–3
John 13:21–32

Thursday 28 March

Exodus 12:1–4 [5–10] 11–14
Psalm 116:1, 10–end [or 116:9 end]
1 Corinthians 11:23–26
John 13:1–17, 31b–35

Friday 29 March

Isaiah 52:13—end of 53
Psalm 22 [or 22:1–11 or 22:1–21]
Hebrews 10:16–25
John 18:1—end of 19

Saturday 30 March

Job 14:1–14
Psalm 31:1–4, 15–16
1 Peter 4:1–8
Matthew 27:57–66

Sunday 31 March

Acts 10:34–43
Isaiah 65:17–end
Psalm 118:1–2, 14–24
1 Corinthians 15:19–26
John 20:1–18
Luke 24:1–12

Monday 1 April

Acts 2:14, 22–32
Psalm 16:1–2, 6–end
Matthew 28:8–15

Tuesday 2 April

Acts 2:36–41
Psalm 33:4–5, 18–end
John 20:11–18

Wednesday 3 April

Acts 3:1–10
Psalm 105:1–9
Luke 24:13–35

Thursday 4 April

Acts 3:11–end
Psalm 8
Luke 24:35–48

Friday 5 April

Acts 4:1–12
Psalm 118:1–4, 22–26
John 21:1–14

Saturday 6 April

Acts 4:13–21
Psalm 118:1–4, 14–21
Mark 16:9–15

Sunday 7 April

Exodus 14:10–end; 15:20–21
Acts 5:27–32
Psalm 118:14–end
Revelation 1:4–8
John 20:19–end

Monday 8 April

Isaiah 7:10–14
Psalm 40:5–11
Hebrews 10:4–10
Luke 1:26–38

Tuesday 9 April

Acts 4:32–end
Psalm 93
John 3:7–15

Wednesday 10 April

Acts 5:17–26
Psalm 34:1–8
John 3:16–21

Thursday 11 April

Acts 5:27–33
Psalm 34:1, 15–end
John 3:31–end

Friday 12 April

Acts 5:34–42
Psalm 27:1–5, 16–17
John 6:1–15

Saturday 13 April

Acts 6:1–7
Psalm 33:1–5, 18–19
John 6:16–21

Sunday 14 April

Zephaniah 3:14–end
Acts 9:1–6
Psalm 30
Revelation 5:11–end
John 21:1–19

Monday 15 April

Acts 6:8–15
Psalm 119:17–24
John 6:22–29

Tuesday 16 April

Acts 7:51–81*a*
Psalm 31:1–5, 16
Deuteronomy 5:22–end
John 6:30–35

Wednesday 17 April

Acts 8:1*b*–8
Psalm 66:1–6
John 6:35–40

Thursday 18 April

Acts 8:26–end
Psalm 66:7–8, 14–end
John 6:44–51

Friday 19 April

Acts 9:1–20
Psalm 117
John 6:52–59

Saturday 20 April

Acts 9:31–42
Psalm 116:10–15
John 6:60–69

Sunday 21 April

Genesis 7:1–5, 11–18
Acts 9:36–end
Psalm 23
Revelation 7:9–end
John 10:22–30

Monday 22 April

Acts 11:1–18
Psalms 42:1–2, 43:1–4
John 10:1–10 (*or* 11–18)

Tuesday 23 April

Revelation 12:7–12
Psalm 126
2 Timothy 2:3–13
John 15:18–21

Wednesday 24 April

Acts 12:24 — 13:5
Psalm 67
John 12:44–end

Thursday 25 April

Proverbs 15:28–end
Psalm 119:9–16
Ephesians 4:7–16
Mark 13:5–13

Friday 26 April

Acts 13:26–33
Psalm 2
John 14:1–6

Saturday 27 April

Acts 13:44–end
Psalm 98:1–5
John 14:7–14

Sunday 28 April

Genesis 22:1–18
Psalm 148
Revelation 21:1–6
John 13:31–35

Monday 29 April

Acts 14:5–18
Acts 1, 11–18
Psalm 118:1–3, 14–15
John 14:21–26

Tuesday 30 April

Acts 14:19–end
Psalm 145:10–end
John 14:27

Wednesday 1 May

Isaiah 30:15–21
Psalm 119:1–8
Ephesians 1:3–10
John 14:1–14

Thursday 2 May

Acts 15:7–21
Psalm 96:1–3, 7–10
John 15:9–11

Friday 3 May

Acts 15:22–31
Psalm 57:8–end
John 15:12–17

Saturday 4 May

Acts 16:1–10
Psalm 100

John 15:18–21
2 Corinthians 4:5–12

Sunday 5 May
Ezekiel 37:1–14
Acts 16:9–15
Psalm 67
Revelation 21:10, 22 — 22:5
John 14:23–29

Monday 6 May
Acts 16:11–15
Psalm 149:1–5
John 15:26 — 16:4

Tuesday 7 May
Acts 16:22–34
Psalm 138
John 16:5–11

Wednesday 8 May
Acts 17:15, 22 — 18:1
Psalm 148:1–2, 11–end
John 16:12–15

Thursday 9 May
Daniel 7:9–14
Psalm 47
Ephesians 1:15–end *or*
    Acts 1:1–11
Luke 24:44–end

Friday 10 May
Acts 18:9–18
Psalm 47:1–6
John 16:20–23

Saturday 11 May
Acts 18:22–end
Psalm 47:1–2, 7–end
John 16:23–28

Sunday 12 May
Ezekiel 36:24–28
Acts 16:16–34
Psalm 97
Revelation 22:12–14, 16–17, 20–
    end
John 17:20–end

Monday 13 May
Acts 19:1–8
Psalm 68:1–6
John 16:29–end

Tuesday 14 May
Isaiah 22:15–end
Acts 1:15–end
Psalm 15
John 15:9–17

Wednesday 15 May
Acts 20:28–end
Psalm 68:27–28, 32–end
John 17:11–19

Thursday 16 May
Acts 22:30 — 23:6–11
Psalm 16:1, 5–end
John 17:20–end

Friday 17 May
Acts 25:13–21
Psalm 103:1–2, 11–12, 19–20
John 21:15–19

Saturday 18 May
Acts 28:16–20, 30–end
Psalm 11:4–end
John 21:20–end

Sunday 19 May
Acts 2:1–21
Genesis 11:1–9
Psalm 104:26–36, 37b
Romans 8:14–17
John 14:8–17 (25–27)

Monday 20 May
James 1:1–11
Psalm 93 *or* 119:65–72
Mark 9:14–29

Tuesday 21 May
James 1:12–18
Psalm 37:3–6, 27–28
Romans 1:18–end
Luke 9:28–36
Mark 9:30–37

Wednesday 22 May
James 1:19–end
Job 3
Joshua 3
Psalm 119:161–168
Mark 9:38–40

Thursday 23 May

James 2:1–9
Psalm 1
Mark 9:41–end

Friday 24 May

James 2:14–24, 26
Psalm 119:19–24
Mark 10:1–12

Saturday 25 May

James 3:1–10
Psalm 103:13–18
Mark 10:13–16

Sunday 26 May

Proverbs 8:1–4, 22–31
Psalm 8
Romans 5:1–5
John 16:12–15

Monday 27 May

James 3:13–end
Psalm 32:1–8
Mark 10:17–27

Tuesday 28 May

James 4:1–10
Psalm 50:1–6
Mark 10:28–31

Wednesday 29 May

James 4:13–end
Psalm 79:8–9, 12, 14
Mark 10:32–45

Thursday 30 May

Genesis 14:18–20
Psalm 116:10–end
1 Corinthians 11, 23–26
John 6:51–58

Or **Thursday 30 May**

James 5:1–6
Psalm 33:1–9
Mark 10:46–end

Friday 31 May

Zephaniah 3:14–18
Psalm 113
Romans 12:9–16
Luke 1:39–49 [50–56]

Saturday 1 June

James 5:13–end
Psalm 19:7–end
Mark 11:27–end

Sunday 2 June

1 Kings 8:22–23, 41–43
Psalm 96
Galatians 1:1–12
Luke 7:1–10

Monday 3 June

1 Peter 1:3–9
Psalm 15
Mark 12:1–12

Tuesday 4 June

1 Peter 1:10–16
Psalm 112
Mark 12:13–17

Wednesday 5 June

1 Peter 1:18–25
Psalm 25:1–8
Mark 12:18–27

Thursday 6 June

1 Peter 2:2–5, 9–12
Psalm 128
Mark 12:28–34

Friday 7 June

1 Peter 4:7–13
Psalm 146
Mark 12:35–37

Saturday 8 June

Jude 17, 20–25
Psalm 103:1, 8–13
Mark 12:38–end

Sunday 9 June

1 Kings 17:17–24
Psalm 146
Galatians 1:11–end
Luke 7:11–17

Monday 10 June

2 Corinthians 1:1–7
Psalm 34:1–8
Matthew 5:1–12

Tuesday 11 June

Job 29:11–16
Psalm 112
Acts 11:19–end
Galatians 2:1–10
John 15:12–17

Wednesday 12 June

2 Corinthians 3:4–11
Psalm 78:1–4
Matthew 5:17–19

Thursday 13 June

2 Corinthians 3:15—4:1, 3–6
Psalm 78:36–40
Matthew 5:20–26

Friday 14 June

2 Corinthians 4:7–15
Psalm 99
Matthew 5:27–32

Saturday 15 June

2 Corinthians 5:14–end
Psalm 103:1–12
Matthew 5:33–37

Sunday 16 June

2 Samuel 11:26–12:10, 13–15
Psalm 5:1–8
Galatians 2:15–end
Luke 7:36—8:3

Monday 17 June

2 Corinthians 6:1–10
Psalm 98
Job 27
Matthew 5:38–42

Tuesday 18 June

2 Corinthians 8:1–9
Psalm 146
Matthew 5:43–end

Wednesday 19 June

2 Corinthians 9:6–11
Psalm 112
Matthew 6:1–6, 16–18

Thursday 20 June

2 Corinthians 11:1–11
Psalm 111
Matthew 6:7–15

Friday 21 June

2 Corinthians 11:18, 21b–30
Psalm 34:1–6
Matthew 6:19–23

Saturday 22 June

2 Corinthians 12:1–10
Psalm 89:20–33
Matthew 6:24–end

Sunday 23 June

Isaiah 65:1–9
Psalms 42, 43
Galatians 3:23–end
Luke 8:26–39

Monday 24 June

Isaiah 40:1–11
Psalm 85:7–end
Galatians 3:23–end
Luke 1:57–66, 80

Tuesday 25 June

Genesis 13:2, 5–end
Psalm 15
Matthew 7:6, 12–14

Wednesday 26 June

Genesis 15:1–12, 17–18
Psalm 105:1–9
Matthew 7:15–20

Thursday 27 June

Genesis 16:1–12, 15–16
Psalm 106:1–5
Matthew 7:21–end

Friday 28 June

Genesis 17:1, 9–10, 15–22
Psalm 128
Matthew 8:1–4

Saturday 29 June

Ezekiel 3:22–end
or Acts 12:1–11
Psalm 125
1 Peter 2:19–end
Matthew 16:13–19

Sunday 30 June

1 Kings 19:5–16, 19–end
Psalm 77:1–2, 11–end
Galatians 5:1, 13–25
Luke 9:51–end

Monday 1 July

Genesis 18:16–end
Psalm 103:6–17
Matthew 8:18–22

Tuesday 2 July

Genesis 19:15–29
Psalm 26
Matthew 8:23–27

Wednesday 3 July

Habakkuk 2:1–4
Psalm 31:1–6
Ephesians 2:19–end
John 20:24–29

Thursday 4 July

Genesis 22:1–19
Psalm 116:1–7
Matthew 9:1–8

Friday 5 July

Genesis 23:1–4, 19 — 24:1–8, 62–
end
Psalm 106:1–5
Matthew 9:9–13

Saturday 6 July

Genesis 27:1–5*a*, 15–29
Psalm 135:1–6
Matthew 9:14–17

Sunday 7 July

Psalm 30
Isaiah 66:10–14
Galatians 6:[1–6] 7–16
Luke 10:1–11, 16–20

Monday 8 July

Genesis 28:10–end
Psalm 91:1–10
Matthew 9:18–26

Tuesday 9 July

Genesis 32:22–end
Psalm 17:1–8
Matthew 9:32–end

Wednesday 10 July

Genesis 41:55–end; 42:5–7, 17–
end
Psalm 33:1–4, 18–end
Matthew 10:1–7

Thursday 11 July

Genesis 44:18–21, 23–29 — 45:1–5
Psalm 105:11–17
Matthew 10:7–15

Friday 12 July

Genesis 46:1–7, 28–30
Psalm 37:3–6, 27–28
Matthew 10:16–23

Saturday 13 July

Genesis 49:29–end; 50:15–25
Psalm 105:1–7
Matthew 10:24–33

Sunday 14 July

Psalm 82
Deuteronomy 30:9–14
Colossians 1:1–14
Luke 10:25–37

Monday 15 July

Exodus 1:8–14, 22
Psalm 124
Matthew 10:34 — 11:1

Tuesday 16 July

Exodus 2:1–15
Psalm 69:1–2, 31–end
Matthew 11:20–24

Wednesday 17 July

Exodus 3:1–6, 9–12
Psalm 103:1–7
Matthew 11:25–27

Thursday 18 July

Exodus 3:13–20
Psalm 105:1–2, 23
Matthew 11:28–end

Friday 19 July

Exodus 11:10 — 12:14
Psalm 116:10–end
Matthew 12:1–8

Saturday 20 July

Exodus 12:37–42
Psalm 136:1–4, 10–15
Matthew 12:14–21

Sunday 21 July
Psalm 52
Genesis 18:1–10a
Colossians 1:15–28
Luke 10:38–end

Monday 22 July
Song of Solomon 3:1–4
Psalm 42:1–10
2 Corinthians 5:14–17
John 20:1–2, 11–18

Tuesday 23 July
Exodus 14:21 — 15:1
Psalm 105:37–44
Matthew 12:46–end

Wednesday 24 July
Exodus 16:1–5, 9–15
Psalm 78:17–31
Matthew 13:1–9

Thursday 25 July
Jeremiah 45:1–5
Psalm 126
Acts 11:27 — 12:2
Matthew 20:20–28

Friday 26 July
Exodus 20:1–17
Psalm 19:7–11
Matthew 13:18–23
Romans 8:28–30

Saturday 27 July
Exodus 24:3–8
Psalm 50:1–6, 14–15
Matthew 13:24–30

Sunday 28 July
Genesis 18:20–32
Psalm 85
Colossians 2:6–15 [16–19]
Luke 11:1–13

Monday 29 July
Exodus 32:15–24, 30–34
Psalm 106:19–23
Matthew 13:31–35
John 12:1–8

Tuesday 30 July
Exodus 33:7–11; 34:5–9, 28
Psalm 103:8–12
Ezekiel 37:15–end
Matthew 13:36–43

Wednesday 31 July
Exodus 34:29–end
Psalm 99
Matthew 13:44–46

Thursday 1 August
Exodus 40:16–21, 34–end
Psalm 84:1–6
Matthew 13:47–53

Friday 2 August
Leviticus 23:1, 4–11, 15–16, 27,
    34–37
Psalm 81:1–8
Matthew 13:54–end

Saturday 3 August
Leviticus 25:1, 8–17
Psalm 67
Matthew 14:1–12

Sunday 4 August
Ecclesiastes 1:2
Psalm 107:1–9, 43 12–14; 2:18–23
Colossians 3:1–11
Luke 12:13–21

Monday 5 August
Numbers 11:4–15
Psalm 81:11–end
Matthew 14:13–21 or 14:22

Tuesday 6 August
Daniel 7:9–10, 13–14
Psalm 97
2 Peter 1:16–19
Luke 9:28–36

Wednesday 7 August
Numbers 13:1–2, 25 — 14:1, 26–35
Psalm 106:14–24
Matthew 15:21–28

Thursday 8 August
Numbers 20:1–13
Psalm 95:1, 8–end
Matthew 16:13–23

Friday 9 August

Deuteronomy 4:32–40
Psalm 77:11–end
Matthew 16:24–end

Saturday 10 August

Deuteronomy 6:4–13
Psalm 18:1–2, 48–end
Matthew 17:14–20

Sunday 11 August

Genesis 15:1–6
Psalm 50:1–8, 23–end
Hebrews 11:1–3, 8–16
Luke 12:32–40

Monday 12 August

Deuteronomy 10:12–end
Psalm 147:13–end
Matthew 17:22–end

Tuesday 13 August

Deuteronomy 31:1–8
Psalm 107:1–3, 42–end
Matthew 18:1–5, 10, 12–14

Wednesday 14 August

Deuteronomy 34
Psalm 66:14–end
Matthew 18:15–20

Thursday 15 August

Isaiah 61:10–end
Psalm 45:10–end
Galatians 4:4–7
Luke 1:46–55

Friday 16 August

Joshua 24:1–13
Psalm 136:1–3, 16–22
Matthew 19:3–12

Saturday 17 August

Joshua 24:14–29
Psalm 16:1, 5–end
Matthew 19:13–15

Sunday 18 August

Jeremiah 23:23–29
Psalm 80:1–2, 9–end
Hebrews 11:29 — 12:2
Luke 12:49–56

Monday 19 August

Judges 2:11–19
Psalm 106:34–42
Matthew 19:16–22

Tuesday 20 August

Judges 6:11–24
Psalm 85:8–end
Matthew 19:23–end

Wednesday 21 August

Judges 9:6–15
Psalm 21:1–6
Matthew 20:1–16

Thursday 22 August

Judges 11:29–end
Psalm 40:4–11
Matthew 22:1–14

Friday 23 August

Ruth 1:1, 3–6, 14–16, 22
Psalm 146
Matthew 22:34–40

Saturday 24 August

Isaiah 43:8–13
Psalm 145:1–7
Acts 5:12–16
Corinthians 4:9–15
Luke 22:24–30

Sunday 25 August

Jeremiah 1:4–10
Isaiah 58:9b–end
Psalm 71:1–6
Hebrews 12:18–end
Luke 13:10–17

Monday 26 August

1 Thessalonians 1:1–5, 8–end
Psalm 149:1–5
Matthew 23:13–22

Tuesday 27 August

1 Thessalonians 2:1–8
Psalm 139:1–9
Matthew 23:23–26

Wednesday 28 August

1 Thessalonians 2:9–13
Psalm 126
Matthew 23:27–32

Thursday 29 August

1 Thessalonians 3:7–end
Psalm 90:13–end
Matthew 24:42–end

Friday 30 August

1 Thessalonians 4:1–8
Psalm 97
Matthew 25:1–13

Saturday 31 August

1 Thessalonians 4:9–12
Psalm 98:1–2, 8–end
Matthew 25:14–30

Sunday 1 September

Jeremiah 2:4–13
Psalm 81:1, 10–end
Hebrews 13:1–8, 15–16
Luke 14:1, 7–14

Monday 2 September

1 Thessalonians 4:13–end
Psalm 96
Luke 4:16–30

Tuesday 3 September

1 Thessalonians 5:1–6, 9–11
Psalm 27:1–8
Luke 4:31–37

Wednesday 4 September

Colossians 1:1–8
Psalm 34:11–18
Luke 4:38–end

Thursday 5 September

Colossians 1:9–14
Psalm 98:1–5
Luke 5:1–11

Friday 6 September

Colossians 1:15–20
Psalm 89:19b–28
Luke 5:33–end

Saturday 7 September

Colossians 1:21–23
Psalm 117
Luke 6:1–5

Sunday 8 September

Psalm 139:1–5, 12–18
Deuteronomy 30:15–end
Philemon 1–21
Luke 14:25–33

Monday 9 September

Colossians 1:24 — 2:3
Psalm 62:1–7
Luke 6:6–11

Tuesday 10 September

Colossians 2:6–15
Psalm 8
Luke 6:12–19

Wednesday 11 September

Colossians 3:1–11
Psalm 15
Luke 6:20–26

Thursday 12 September

Colossians 3:12–17
Psalm 149:1–5
Luke 6:27–38

Friday 13 September

1 Timothy 1:1–2, 12–14
Psalm 16
Luke 6:39–42

Saturday 14 September

Numbers 21:4–9
Psalm 22:23–28
Philippians 2:6–11
John 3:13–17

Sunday 15 September

Jeremiah 4:11–12, 22–28
Psalm 14
1 Timothy 1:12–17
Luke 15:1–10

Monday 16 September

1 Timothy 2:1–8
Psalm 28
Luke 7:1–10

Tuesday 17 September

1 Timothy 3:1–13
Psalm 101
Luke 7:11–17

Wednesday 18 September
1 Timothy 3:14–end
Psalm 111:1–5
Luke 7:31–35

Thursday 19 September
1 Timothy 4:12–end
Psalm 111:6–end
Luke 7:36–end

Friday 20 September
1 Timothy 6:2–12
Psalm 49:1–9
Luke 8:1–3

Saturday 21 September
Proverbs 3:13–18
Psalm 119:65–72
2 Corinthians 4:1–6
Matthew 9:9–13

Sunday 22 September
Jeremiah 8:18—9:1
Psalm 79:1–9
1 Timothy 2:1–7
Luke 16:1–13

Monday 23 September
Ezra 1:1–6
Psalm 126
Luke 8:16–18

Tuesday 24 September
Ezra 6:7–8, 12, 14–20
Psalm 124
Luke 8:19–21

Wednesday 25 September
Ezra 9:5–9
Psalm 77
Luke 9:1–6

Thursday 26 September
Haggai 1:1–8
Psalm 149:1–5
Luke 9:7–9

Friday 27 September
Haggai 1:15b—2:9
Psalm 43
Luke 9:18–22

Saturday 28 September
Zechariah 2:1–5, 10–11
Psalm 125
Luke 9:43b–45

Sunday 29 September
Genesis 28:10–17
Psalm 103:19–end
Revelation 12:7–12
John 1:47–end

Monday 30 September
Zechariah 8:1–8
Psalm 102:12–22
Luke 9:46–50

Tuesday 1 October
Zechariah 8:20–end
Psalms 87
Luke 9:51–56

Wednesday 2 October
Nehemiah 2:1–8
Psalm 137:1–6
Luke 9:57–end

Thursday 3 October
Nehemiah 8:1–12
Psalm 19:7–11
Luke 10:1–12

Friday 4 October
Deuteronomy 31:7–13
Psalm 79:1–9
Luke 10:13–16

Saturday 5 October
Joshua 22:1–6
Psalm 69:33–37
Luke 10:17–24

Sunday 6 October
Lamentations 1:1–6
Psalm 137
2 Timothy 1:1–14
Luke 17:5–10

Monday 7 October
Jonah 1:1–2:2, 10
Psalm 69:1–6
Luke 10:25–37

Tuesday 8 October
Jonah 3
Psalm 130
Luke 10:38–end

Wednesday 9 October
Jonah 4
Psalm 86:1–9
Luke 11:1–4

Thursday 10 October
Malachi 3:13 — 4:2a
Psalm 1
Luke 11:5–13

Friday 11 October
Joel 1:13–15; 2:1–2
Psalm 9:1–7
Luke 11:15–26

Saturday 12 October
Joel 3:12–end
Psalm 97:1, 8–end
Luke 11:27–28

Sunday 13 October
Jeremiah 29:1, 4–7
Psalm 66:1–11
2 Timothy 2:8–15
Luke 17:11–19

Monday 14 October
Romans 1:1–7
Psalm 98
Luke 11:29–32

Tuesday 15 October
Romans 1:16–25
Psalm 19:1–4
Luke 11:37–41

Wednesday 16 October
Romans 2:1–11
Psalm 62:1–8
Luke 11:42–46

Thursday 17 October
Romans 3:21–30
Psalm 130
Luke 11:47–end

Friday 18 October
Isaiah 35:3–6
Psalm 147:1–7
2 Timothy 4:5–17
Luke 10:1–9

Saturday 19 October
Romans 4:13, 16–18
Psalm 105:6–10, 41–44
Luke 12:8–12

Sunday 20 October
Jeremiah 31:27–34
Psalm 119:97–104
2 Timothy 3:14 — 4:5
Luke 18:1–8

Monday 21 October
Romans 4:20–end
Psalms 123
Luke 12:13–21
Micah 1:1–9

Tuesday 22 October
Romans 5:12, 15, 17–end
Psalm 40:7–12
Luke 12:35–38
Micah 2

Wednesday 23 October
Romans 6:12–18
Psalm 124
Luke 12:39–48
Micah 3

Thursday 24 October
Romans 6:19–end
Psalm 1
Luke 12:49–53

Friday 25 October
Romans 7:18–end
Psalm 119:33–40
Luke 12:54–end

Saturday 26 October
Romans 8:1–11
Psalm 24:1–6
Luke 13:1–9

Sunday 27 October
Joel 2:23–end
Psalm 65
2 Timothy 4:6–8, 16–18
Luke 18:9–14

Or **Sunday 27 October**
Isaiah 45:22–end
Psalm 119:129–136
Romans 15:1–6
Luke 4:16–24

Monday 28 October
Isaiah 28:14–16
Psalm 119:89–96
Ephesians 2:19–end
John 15:17–end

Tuesday 29 October
Romans 8:18–25
Psalm 126
Luke 13:18–21

Wednesday 30 October
Romans 8:26–30
Psalm 13
Luke 13:22–30
Habakkuk 1:1–11

Thursday 31 October
Romans 8:31–end
Psalm 109:20–26, 29–30
Luke 13:31–end
Habakkuk 1:12—2:5

Or **Friday 1 November**
Isaiah 56:3–8
Psalm 33:1–5
Hebrews 12:18–24
Matthew 5:1–12
Habakkuk 2:6–end

Saturday 2 November
Romans 11:1–2, 11–12, 25–29
Psalm 94:14–19
Luke 14:1, 7
Habakkuk 3:2–19a

Sunday 3 November
Isaiah 1:10–18
Psalm 32:1–8
2 Thessalonians 1
Luke 19:1–10

Monday 4 November
Romans 11:29–end
Psalm 69:31–37
Isaiah 1:1–20
Luke 14:12–14

Tuesday 5 November
Romans 12:5–16
Psalm 131
Luke 14:15–24

Wednesday 6 November
Romans 13:8–10
Psalm 112
Luke 14:25–33

Thursday 7 November
Romans 14:7–12
Psalm 27:14–end
Isaiah 2:12–end
Luke 15:1–10

Friday 8 November
Romans 15:14–21
Psalm 98
Isaiah 3:1–5
Luke 16:1–8

Saturday 9 November
Romans 16:3–9, 16, 22–end
Psalm 145:1–7
Luke 16:9–15
Isaiah 4:2–5:7

Sunday 10 November
Job 19:23–27*a*
Psalm 17:1–9
2 Thessalonians 2:1–5, 13–end
Luke 20:27–38

Monday 11 November
Titus 1:1–9
Psalm 139:1–9 *or* 24:1–6
Luke 17:1–6
Isaiah 5:25–end

Tuesday 12 November
Titus 2:1–8, 11–14
Psalm 34:1–6; 37:3–5, 30–32
Luke 17:7–10
Isaiah 5:25–end

Wednesday 13 November
Titus 3:1–7
Psalm 82 or 23
Matthew 5:21–37
Luke 17:11–19
Isaiah 6

Thursday 14 November
Philemon 7–20
Isaiah 7:1–17
Psalm 119:89–96 or 146:4–end
Luke 17:20–25

Friday 15 November
2 John 4–9
Psalm 19:1–4 or 119:1–8
Luke 17:26–end
Isaiah 8:16–97

Saturday 16 November
3 John 5–8
Psalm 105:1–5, 35–42 or 112
Luke 18:1–8
Isaiah 8:16—9:7

Sunday 17 November
Malachi 4:1–2a
Psalm 98
2 Thessalonians 3:6–13
Luke 21:5–19

Monday 18 November
Revelation 1:1–4; 2:1–5
Psalm 79:1–5
Luke 18:35–end
Isaiah 9:8—10:4

Tuesday 19 November
Revelation 3:1–6, 14–31
Psalm 11 or 15
Luke 19:1–10
Isaiah 10:5–19

Wednesday 20 November
Revelation 4
Psalm 116:10–end or 150
Luke 19:11–28
Isaiah 10:20–32

Thursday 21 November
Revelation 5:1–10
Psalm 129 or 149:1–5
Luke 19:41–44
Isaiah 10:33—11:9

Friday 22 November
Revelation 10:8–11
Isaiah 11:10–end of 12
Psalm 122 or 119:65–72
Luke 19:45–48

Saturday 23 November
Revelation 11:4–12
Psalm 124 or 144:1–9
Luke 20:27–40
Isaiah 13:1–13

Sunday 24 November
Jeremiah 23:1–6
Psalm 46
Colossians 1:11–20
Luke 23:33–43

Monday 25 November
Daniel 1:1–6, 8–20
Psalms 92
Isaiah 14:3–20
Luke 21:1–4

Tuesday 26 November
Daniel 2:31–45
Isaiah 17
Luke 21:5–11

Wednesday 27 November
Daniel 5:1–6, 13–14, 16–17, 23–28
Luke 21:12–19
Psalm 110
Isaiah 19

Thursday 28 November
Daniel 6:12–end
Psalms 125
Luke 21:20–28
Isaiah 21:1–12

Friday 29 November
Daniel 7:2–14
Psalm 139
Isaiah 22:1–14
Luke 21:29–33

Saturday 30 November
Isaiah 52:7–10
Psalms 19:1–6
Romans 10:12–18
Matthew 4:18–22

Acknowledgements

Pray Now 2013 was prepared by members of the Pray Now Writing Group: Peggy Roberts, Carol Ford, Tina Kemp, Adam Dillon, Mark Foster, MaryAnn Rennie, Ishbel McFarlane and Graham Fender-Allison.

Daily headline Scripture quotations are taken from the *New Revised Standard Version*, © 1989 Division of Christian Education of the National Council of Churches of Christ in the United States of America, published by Oxford University Press.

The Revised Common Lectionary is copyright © The Consultation on Common Texts, 1992 and is reproduced with permission. The Church of England's adapted form of *The Revised Common Lectionary*, published as the Principal Service Lectionary in *Common Worship: Services and Prayers for the Church of England*, the Second and Third Service Lectionaries and the *Common Worship* Calendar, also published in the same publication, and the Lectionaries for Certain Lesser Festivals, Common of the Saints and Special Occasions, published in the annual *Common Worship Lectionary*, are copyright © The Archbishops' Council of the Church of England, 1995, 1997. The *Common Worship* Weekday Lectionary is copyright © The Archbishops' Council, 2005. Material from these works is reproduced with permission.

With special thanks to Fiona Skellet, Anna Reid, Anne Whyte and Jane Fender-Allison for their assistance in proof reading and editing.

Contact Us

For further information about *Pray Now* and other publications form the Mission and Discipleship Council's Faith Expressions Team, contact:

Faith Expressions Team
Mission and Discipleship Council
Church of Scotland
121 George Street
Edinburgh EH2 4YN

Tel: 0131 225 5722
Fax: 0131 220 3113

e-mail: mand@cofscotland.org.uk

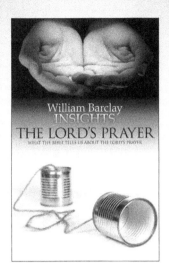

The Lord's Prayer

What the Bible Tells Us about the Lord's Prayer

WILLIAM BARCLAY

Foreword by
RICHARD HARRIES

978-0-7152-0859-5 (paperback)

See our website for details.
www.standrewpress.com

SAINT ANDREW PRESS

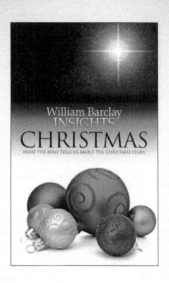

Christmas

What the Bible Tells Us about the Christmas Story

WILLIAM BARCLAY

Foreword by
NICK BAINES

978-0-7152-0858-8 (paperback)

See our website for details.
www.standrewpress.com

SAINT ANDREW PRESS

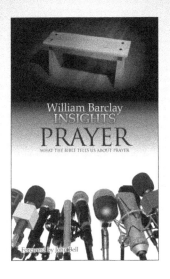

Easter

What the Bible Tells Us about the Easter Story

WILLIAM BARCLAY

Foreword by
DIANE LOUISE JORDAN

978-0-7152-0860-1 (paperback)

See our website for details.
www.standrewpress.com

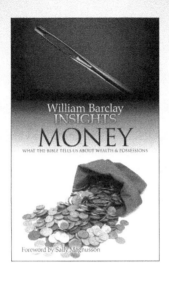